THE SPORTS PHYSIO

ANONYMOUS LADY IN WHITE

FOREWORD

Dearest Readers,

Hello, and a warm welcome to my raunchy account of life as a leading sports physiotherapist.

I've worked with international footballers and rugby players and tended to the needs of Olympians and heavy-weight boxers from across the globe (I'm looking at you - USA, Australia, New Zealand and Jamaica). And...as I will confess in these pages...I've been intimate with many of them.

I've worked hard to disguise the famous sportsmen featured in these pages, but I've left a few clues in because life's more fun that way.

None of the sportsmen I have been intimate with coerced me or made me do anything I didn't want. Everything that has happened has been consensual. Perhaps I'm just highly sexed, or perhaps it's the thought of rough hands on soft thighs and the feeling of big hands pulling open my blouse and caressing my large breasts. I find it a real turn-on.

I suppose the fact that my job involves hands-on touching… with oils… on a bed…with a sportsman wearing little more than a tiny towel makes it more likely that something will happen. I just help by wearing an incredibly short, tight uniform and smiling provocatively.

There's no question that I should have been more professional. I should have swatted away the manly advances, but I didn't. Not one of them. Christ, I've had some fun. And I think it's about time I shared some of the delicious details with you.

Brace yourselves. We are going on quite a ride….

The Anonymous Lady in White xx

NOTE: I have not slowed down the text with descriptions about contraception, but I always practised safe sex (and so should you!)

TONGUES, TITS & TEASING:
HOW IT ALL BEGAN

The first time it happened, it was by accident. Well, I say 'accident.' It's not as if I hadn't thought about it before…many times. It had been on my mind since I started working as a trainee sports physiotherapist for a group of handsome, fit, large men who were bursting with testosterone. I mean - come on. I was 20 years old. Who wouldn't have thought about it?

I was at university at the time, training to be a physiotherapist and right from the beginning of my course, I'd told them that I wanted to specialise in sport, so when the time came to go on a block release course in the community, I was assigned to a local rugby club.

I was doing quite low-level work, but I didn't

care. I was working in sport, and that was all I cared about. I would do whatever was asked of me.

On this particular day, I had to massage a guy for a recent shoulder injury as part of his rehab.

I hadn't got to know the player who I'd be massaging very well during my eight-week work experience stint. He wasn't a man who went in for small talk. He hadn't come over and spoken to me like the other men had. This guy - let's call him Mike - had kept himself to himself and had seemed immune to my feminine charms. That made him more exciting. His cold indifference turned me on. It made me feel like he'd be a conquest...someone to strive for. I wasn't as attracted to the guys who always hung around me. This guy was the one I'd taken a fancy to.

So, I felt a shiver of excitement when he came into my small, make-shift surgery. He'd had a nasty injury that had required an operation and some time away from the game; now he was in rehab, starting to do light training and getting himself fit to play.

He'd done a quick session without contact, and I'd been asked to give him an all-over deep tissue massage and check out the shoulder for range of movement.

"Take some of the tension away," the doctor had said.

I certainly did that. By the time I'd finished, the tension had well and truly gone...dissipated into the early evening air along with the smell of lust and satisfaction.

"Where do you want me?" he said when he walked into the room in the tiniest towel. He didn't say hello, and he didn't make eye contact.

"Just on the bed there, please. Face down," I said, feeling a tingle of lust rush through me as he dropped his towel. He had a gorgeous body. Still wet from the shower, he looked tremendous, with a huge chest covered in hair and broad muscley shoulders, with a big scar down one of them.

I began by gently easing out the shoulder, very lightly, to get the blood circulating and to feel around and check what state the scar tissue was in. It was better than I expected. It needed work but was healing well.

I smiled down at Mike as he watched me working on his shoulder. He winked as I smiled, and his whole face lit up. He wasn't classically handsome but had a rough, untamed look that I loved. Square chin, stubbly, big legs, huge chest, eyes that screamed 'fuck me...'

I like Harry Styles as much as the next woman, and I think the boys from Westlife are lovely, but - boy - I'll take a big man with giant thighs over all of them, any time.

Mike and I started chatting, and he told me about his injury and various other injuries he'd acquired through his sport. I told him some ways to avoid them (much more flexibility work) and what to do immediately after getting injured (ice, ice and more ice).

"How are you finding it, working in rugby?" he asked.

"I'm enjoying it. You're all keeping me very busy."

"Are the guys all OK with you? We don't get too many women working with the team. No - let's change that - we don't get any women working with the team."

"The players have been fine. No problems at all."

"You know they all fancy you, don't you? You must realise that."

"What? Me? No, they don't."

"Of course, they do. You're so attractive, I bet all the men you meet fancy you."

I smiled at him again, and he smiled back. Our eyes met, and a spark of pure lust dazzled between us.

"I certainly do," he said.

I could feel my heart beating a little faster, I felt all hot and flustered. I wanted to kiss him all the way down his back and tear the little towel off him with my teeth.

"Everything OK?" he asked. "You look miles away."

"Yep - just thinking…"

Mike had his arms resting on the bed, his palms facing up. He had such big hands that I kept thinking about what they would feel like on me. As I massaged him, I leaned over and gently brushed against his hands.

He didn't flinch.

I wasn't sure what to do. I wanted this man, but I was a professional - I couldn't turn him over and mount him.

"Sorry," I said. "I didn't mean to brush against you like that."

I tried hard not to let the lust show in my voice as I spoke to him. I tried to steady myself and stay professional, but I was all flustered.

"It's quite hot in here, isn't it?" I said.

I know. I know. I was being obvious.

"It's very hot," he said. "And, by the way, any time you want to brush against me - just go ahead."

"I'll bear that in mind," I said. As I leaned over to massage him again, he lifted his hand and stroked my thigh. "Is this OK?" he asked.

I could hardly speak. "It's fine," I said.

He moved his hand higher. "Still OK?" His hand was practically touching the lace edging of my panties. It was fine, I was loving it, but I couldn't speak. I felt so horny I could hardly breathe.

"If you still feel hot, you could remove some clothes," he said.

I don't think he expected me to, but I undid the first two poppers at the top of my uniform. I had very large breasts. They annoyed me when I was much younger because I could never find anything to fit. But I grew to enjoy them. I enjoyed the look on men's faces when they saw me.

I enjoyed the look on Mike's face when he saw my curves, sitting in a lacy bra. Two large, soft and silky breasts making an escape from the top of my uniform.

He turned around and sat up. "Come here," he said, his voice deeper and gravellier than before. He grabbed my uniform and pulled the rest of it open. I sighed so loudly he could tell instantly how much I wanted him. Then his hands were on my breasts, pulling my bra off so they bounced free. He muttered a sigh from deep within him and pulled me down onto him, sucking my breasts. I could feel his rough skin all over my chest.

He pulled the towel away and had a huge erection.

I took it in my hands and caressed it. I could feel myself get wet as he circled his tongue around my nipples, his hands travelling down and tearing off my knickers.

"Oh my God," he said. "You're so sexy." And he slid his large fingers inside me.

Oh God, it was gorgeous.

I opened my legs as far as they could go so his hands could get right inside me, and I pushed against his fingers, which were rubbing gently on my clitoris, rubbing and rubbing until I came. Oh God, it was wonderful.

"Your turn," I said, instructing him to sit on the bed facing me. I fell to my knees and took his huge cock in my mouth, holding his balls as I sucked and licked; I felt horny again as he pushed into me harder and faster, close to coming.

"On the floor," he said, stepping off the bed. I lay down, and he kissed and sucked my nipples, fondling my clit, while he bit lightly on my breasts. I was desperate for him to be inside me.

"Now," I said. "Please, I want you inside me."

He pushed himself inside me, staring into my eyes

as he fucked me. He pushed harder, moaned loudly, and then came.

"Christ, that was good," he said.

"It was lovely," I said. "Now, shall I take a look at that shoulder?"

THE RETURN OF THE SEXY
RUGBY PLAYER

I thought I should tell you a little more about myself before proceeding further with this tale of lustful adventure. I went to an ordinary school and did reasonably well in my exams, but nothing special. If I had been brighter, I would have been a doctor. I was always interested in medicine, but I didn't fancy being a nurse. They seemed to do all the grunt work for none of the glory, and so much of their work wasn't 'hands-on'. I wanted to get stuck in and make people better.

I was always very sporty, so the idea of becoming a sports physiotherapist appealed to me.

In case you don't know much about sports physios, they are health professionals who diagnose and treat sports injuries and help athletes prevent and recover from injuries. Physios are kind of like the first line of defence...hovering on the sidelines at matches and picking up the pieces after training. We're the first to spot problems and often the first with a diagnosis. The doctors and surgeons will step in and mend the players, but there's a lot we can do to help players avoid injury, and there's a tonne we can do after injuries to make the recovery as quick as possible.

Some physios work directly for sports clubs; others work in

private practice and deal with sports teams and organisations as part of the practice's work.

To be a good physio, you must use instinct and quick analysis. You need a good knowledge of anatomy, physiology, biomechanics, and psychology.

And getting players to listen to you is easier if you are young, blonde and have very large breasts. I'm sorry if that's not a very feminist thing to say. It's true.

Sport is a very masculine, very highly sexed environment. Large breasts are a definite asset.

I did my degree at a decent university. I won't say which one, but it was approved by the UK Health Professions Council (HPC). I worked hard, learned the theory and practice of physiotherapy, and gained valuable experience in clinical placements.

While at university, I did the rugby club placement as part of my degree course as I mentioned in the first chapter. That was my introduction to the world of sportsmen in a professional environment.

Then a rugby player called Mike came in and - well - you know the rest.

When I returned to college after the eight-week stint at the club, I told a couple of the girls what had happened with Mike, and they sat around listening open-mouthed. They all found it so exciting. Once I'd opened the Pandora's Box, everyone contributed, discussing the gorgeous men we'd met. I was the only one to have taken it further, though.

My friend Caroline had spent her entire work experience with old people. I don't know how she got dealt that short straw, but it made her particularly keen to hear my tale of misadventure.

I must have told the story about a dozen times.

I gloried in it, loved it and entertained myself with it. His huge thighs, the hard cock that I desperately wanted to fuck. Christ.

Every time I talked about him, I felt horny. I'd go to bed with my vibrator and think about it all…those big hands tearing open the front of my dress, me standing there while he watched me. My nipples erect and yearning to be stroked. My pussy - soft and wet. I would cum almost immediately as I thought about it…about him.

The more I fantasised, the more I knew I would do the same thing if I ever found myself in that position again.

Is that bad?

Yes, it is. I could have been struck off. But the wonderful feeling it gave me was out of this world.

I hoped my adventure with Mike showed a healthy interest in the opposite sex.

It's not as if I had sex with the whole team…not at that stage, I didn't. I only had sex with that one man on a delicious day that I knew I'd never be able to get out of my mind.

Then, something marvellous happened.

I was in a lecture when a call came through. It was the rugby club. One of the players wanted me to treat him. They realised that I was back at university now and not obliged to work with the team, but I'd worked on this particular guy's injury when I was there before, and he had found it helpful.

'Sure,' I said. 'I don't mind helping. Why don't I meet him in the physio's room on Tuesday after training?'

'Perfect,' said the guy. 'I'll tell him.'

'Which guy is it, by the way?' I asked.

'Mike Saunders,' said the club official. 'I'll make sure he goes straight there after training.'

Tuesday couldn't come around fast enough.

I had no choice about what I wore to the meeting with Mike. I was there in a professional capacity, after all, but I did have the option of what underwear to wear. I dressed slowly after covering myself in a delicious body lotion, then I slipped into my work uniform and headed for the rugby club physio room, my legs shaking as I attempted to change gear, heart pounding, excitement fizzling through me. I arrived and went to get myself ready.

Mike came in straight from training; he was big, dirty and looked utterly delicious with his lovely, unshaven face and brown eyes burning through me. His coach was standing behind him.

"Is it your shoulder again?" I asked, reaching over to take various instruments from my bag and move them to the bed.

"Yes,' he said, pulling off his shirt. I tried not to gasp at the gorgeous, manly body revealed by his swift movement.

"I just think it needs loosening up," said his coach, a rather gnarly old man called Malcolm. "We need someone who can get right in there and break up the tissue. You don't look like you've got the strength love, but Mike says you have. He says you got right in the last time."

"I'm stronger than I look," I said.

"Okay, I'll leave you to it," said Malcolm. "See you in the bar later, Mike."

Malcolm walked towards the door. "Thanks again, love, you are an absolute lifesaver," he said. He walked out, closing the door behind him, and I followed him and bolted it. I turned around, and Mike was sitting on the edge of the physio's table, staring at me.

"Hello," I said, walking back towards him. "Is your shoulder sore?"

"Not in the least."

"Oh, I see."

Mike stood up and walked towards me, taking my face in his hands and kissing me gently.

"Kiss me harder," I said, so he did… tonguing me with passion and pushing himself up against me, pulling me in tightly, and growling slightly as he removed his lips from mine and kissed me on the cheek.

"Fuck me, you're sexy," he said. "I'd almost forgotten how sexy."

"Talking about forgetful, I think I forgot something too…" I said.

"What?" he asked, kissing all around the edge of my face.

"I forgot all of my underwear," I said. He gave out another of those gorgeous involuntary groans that he did occasionally, which drove me wild.

"That was very forgetful of you," he said, unbuttoning my uniform. I lay my hands on his thighs, moving them up under the edges of his shorts and right up to his groin.

My breasts bounced free of the uniform. "Oh, my God, you were serious; you have no underwear on," he said, and in one quick jolt, he pulled down his shorts and stood before me with a raging erection. He moved his head down to kiss my breasts while he fumbled with the rest of the fastenings on the front of my uniform. I loved his jittery hands; he was so turned on that he could hardly move them properly. Finally, he reached the last one, and my uniform hung open.

"On your hands and knees," he said. I removed the uniform and did as he commanded, opening my thighs as wide as possible. Whenever I do doggy style, I like to have my legs wide; it makes me feel so vulnerable and turned on. He came up behind me and pushed one hand between my legs, gently caressing me, his fingers fumbling around to find my clitoris while his other hand fondled my breasts.

"Oh, God," he said, "I want you so much."

"Get inside me. Get inside right now. I need you inside me."

He didn't have to be asked twice; he pushed his huge penis into me. Oh God, the feeling of being so full of him while he continued to stroke my clitoris and massage my breasts was incredible. He was pushing inside me, the push becoming more urgent, and his fondling of my breasts so rough. Oh, it was lovely. I like it rough. Rubbing and pushing himself into me while those big hands covered me. Oh God. Oh, it was gorgeous. I'd never felt so turned on. "Keep going, keep going," I said, dropping to my elbows and opening my legs wider, feeling myself move towards orgasm. I heard him moan. He was getting there. He thrust and thrust, and I felt a wave of excitement roll through my body.

"Oh God, that feels wonderful," I yelled, moving my hand down to stroke myself along with him. That seemed to turn him on even more, and with one almighty thrust, he was there. He cried out while I felt orgasm run through me again.

"Oh God," I said. "Oh God."

We collapsed down next to each other in the makeshift physio room. Him still covered in mud, me naked and smiling. My uniform lay discarded on the floor.

"How is your shoulder?" I asked.

"Fucking amazing," he said

THE DOCTOR IS CUMMING

I graduated from my physiotherapy course and signed up for a post-graduate diploma in sports physiotherapy. This mixture of classroom and practical, hands-on experience was taking me exactly where I wanted to go.

I also had a part-time job at a big, busy London hospital where I seemed to be involved in everything except the first-response teams. A lot of my work was giving physiotherapy support to those who were recovering from surgery, but I was available to all departments in the hospital...from geriatric to A&E to antenatal. Unlike the doctors and nurses, I didn't have a specialist area.

It was a good job and provided much-needed income and tonnes of experience across hospital disciplines, but I think the main thing I learned was that I never wanted to work in hospitals. The clinical environment, the proximity to serious illness, and the life-and-death decision-making weren't for me.

To be perfectly frank with you, I wasn't strong enough to deal with it. The things that hospital staff see and deal with - mentally and physically - are beyond belief. They are superheroes. Next time you're in hospital, remember to thank them. We are all quick to criticise the NHS, and I know there is much wrong with it, but the vast majority of the people working within its crumbling walls are good, solid, hard-working and committed. I salute you all.

While working at the hospital, I met a doctor in the A&E department. I'd bumped into him several times before and worked with one of his patients, but I didn't know him well. He was always very chatty and friendly, which I liked. Most of the consultants kept themselves to themselves, but this guy – let's call him Andy Clark – was pleasant, friendly and helpful. One day, I bumped into him in the staff room.

"How are you doing?" he asked.

"OK. It's going well. I'm busy all the time," I said.

"If you need any help with anything – just shout."

"Thanks," I replied.

He was a slightly older man, not quite my dad's age, but not far off. He was wiry and intense...tall with greying hair. He wasn't handsome in any conventional sense, but he was very clean-looking and well-presented. He looked like he would fold his clothes neatly after sex, maybe even jump up and rush into the shower straight afterwards and have a range of fragrances lined up on his perfectly clean bathroom shelf. Let's just say he wasn't like the rough and ready sportsmen I tended to go for.

A couple of days after seeing him in the staff room, I caught up with Simone, one of the nurses I'd become friendly with. She was a scrub nurse in the A&E department, so our paths didn't cross professionally, but we bonded soon after I arrived at the hospital through a joint love of pain au chocolat.

"So – you and Doctor Clark, eh?" she said.

"Dr Clark?" I said, wondering what she was talking about.

"Yes – Andy - don't pretend you don't know him; I've seen you talking to him. He's got quite a crush on you."

"Oh, come on," I said.

I kind of knew that he liked me, but it was strange to think of it. He was so "proper" and so shy that I never imagined he would ever do anything about it. I was surprised he would ever mention his "crush" to anyone.

"Why do you say that? Has he said something?" I asked.

"Kind of," said Simone. "He's a really good guy, a really good guy."

I didn't know what to do with that information, so I smiled, told her I'd see her in the morning for a pain au chocolat if she was around, and went on my way.

Was he going to ask me out? How weird would that be? He must be 10 years older than me and looked very much like a confirmed bachelor.

The next time I saw Andy, he was strolling down the corridor with his lambswool sweater thrown prep style over his shoulders.

"Hello there," he said, and I felt myself blush. It wasn't because I fancied him; it was because I knew he fancied me, so I suddenly felt embarrassed in his company.

"I was wondering…" he said, stroking his chin, clearly nervous. "I understand if you're busy because it's not much notice, but do you fancy meeting for dinner one night?"

He hadn't suggested a night, so I don't know why he thought it wasn't much notice.

"I was thinking maybe Friday. Sorry - I should have said that. Friday? Is Friday OK? I understand if it isn't. No worries."

"Sure, I can make Friday," I said. "That would be nice."

"Great, great," he replied, smiling from ear to ear. "This Friday night?"

"Yes, that's fine. I'm free then."

We exchanged numbers, and he kissed me lightly on the cheek. It was a soft, cold, slightly wet kiss that reminded me of young children kissing your face after eating ice cream. It wasn't pleasant, and every part of me wanted to cry off on Friday night, but that seemed utterly ridiculous. Nothing had to happen. I could just go for a pleasant dinner with this pleasant man...that was all. Or so I thought at the time.

I dressed casually for our meeting. I didn't have much choice...I was a poor student with debts after university, so buying fancy clothes wasn't something I could do. But I was young and pretty back then, so able to get away without designer clothing to shore things up for me.

I put on a pair of tight jeans, some strappy gold sandals and a white shirt. I put my hair into a pony-tail, put some gold hoops in my ears, and did my makeup well. I was quite proud of my appearance: casual but composed and elegant. I didn't know quite how much effort he would make, though. I met him at the restaurant he had suggested, a lovely little place on the South Bank near the hospital where we both worked. It had a French vibe, with red and white check tablecloths and candles in bottles. It looked very rustic.

I saw him sitting in the far corner, with his glasses perched on his head and a copy of The Times news-paper on the table. He stood up to greet me, and I could see he was wearing an immaculate suit with a rather dapper handkerchief in the front pocket, which matched his tie.

"You look divine," he said. "Beautiful."

"You look very smart," I replied as he made a jig across the space between us to pull the chair out for me. It was a very lovely gesture, but I always think it's rather odd, this assumption that women can't pull out chairs. I don't mean to mock chivalry, but it's sometimes harder to pull yourself into the table once a man's pulled the chair out for you than it is to just sit down in the first place. Anyway, he did it with the most charming intention, and I smiled warmly at him.

"I've taken the liberty of ordering some wine. Do you like Sancerre?"

I don't think I'd ever heard of it, let alone tasted it, but I didn't want to appear gauche, so I told him it was my favourite, and he smiled as if very pleased with himself for how he was conducting this date.

"So, how are you getting on, then? Come on, tell me everything." We chatted through my role and talked about hospital issues for the entire dinner, with him explaining exactly what he did and why he'd always wanted to be a surgeon. He told me about the staff members, analysing them as medical professionals rather than indulging in any gossipy details about their private lives.

He confessed that he'd liked me since he first saw me but hadn't had the guts to ask me out. We finished the bottle of wine (I'll be honest, I drank most of it) and sat back in our seats. I felt quite nervous in his company as if I was out with one of my dad's friends and they were likely to report back to my dad on how I behaved. Everything about him screamed authority. He didn't seem to relax, giggle or smile for the entire time, but kept telling me how much he was enjoying himself.

The second bottle of wine came, and he told me he better not have any of it because he was operating the following morning. That alarmed me. If I drank it all myself, I'd be under the table. I shared this concern with him. "Oh goodness, no one's expecting you to drink it all yourself. Just have a glass and leave the rest if that's what you fancy."

Has anyone ever done that? Has anyone ever, in the history of restaurants, sent wine back? Anyway, we didn't. I drank most of it, and he eventually decided to have one extra glass; then we stood up, and I sort of stumbled into him, and I don't know how it happened, but I was kissing him, and he was telling me to come back to his flat in town. That seemed like a good idea because I had no idea how to get to my house. Come for a coffee, get yourself sobered up, and I'll get you safely home.

It's all a blur, every part of it. I guess, though, even though he made it obvious that he liked me and practically dragged me back to his flat, I still didn't think anything would happen. He seemed such as sensible, grown-up sort of man. I imagined he might tuck me into bed and read me a story from his copy of the Times…perhaps a story from the science pages.

I'll be honest, though, it wasn't quite like that. He fumbled with the buttons of my shirt, then fumbled so much with the buttons of my jeans that I recall having to remove them myself; then he panted a lot, kissed my breasts, and came all over my stomach.

It was probably for the best.

Then we slumped into bed, and the next morning, when the sunlight streaked through the blinds we'd forgotten to close, I looked over at him, and my heart sank. Why on earth I slept with him? What was I thinking?

I don't mean to insult him; it's just that there was no chance of us having a relationship – we were too different. If the previous evening had proved anything, it was that we were from different worlds. So why did I sleep with him? Especially since I work with him every day.

Luckily, he was an absolute gentleman, and when I said that I had enjoyed his company but thought we should leave it there, he said he understood. He added that he was disappointed and hoped he hadn't done anything to offend me, but he completely understood.

I told him that he hadn't done anything to offend me. It was just that I would be moving on from the hospital soon and didn't want to get into any sort of relationship. I told him I liked him greatly and hoped we could stay friends.

I bumped into him occasionally around the

hospital after that, but I wouldn't say we stayed friends. Then, I didn't see him for decades, until relatively recently, as a senior government advisor. He was a regular face on television discussing the pandemic. He hadn't changed a bit from when I knew him.

A LOVELY, BIG AUSSIE MAN

*O*nce I'd finished my post-grad course, I was
offered a fantastic opportunity to go out to
the Australian Institute of Sport and work with
leading athletes, coaches and medics. The Institute
was the gold medal standard for elite sports training
back then, and countries worldwide were trying to
copy its approach to sport.

Much of Australia's sporting success back then
was attributed to the IOS, and when the offer came
through, I thought it would be great for my CV and
that I'd learn a lot in the process.

I was told that I would be working mainly with
tennis players for the first two months, then I'd be
seconded to look after rugby World Cup players and
spend time with the Australian cricket team.

In addition, I'd be living in the sun and having
barbies on the beach. I couldn't wait.

I was told that I would be leaving in a month, which seemed pretty quick to get myself sorted, help the girls find another flatmate, sort out visas, etc., but a few days after asking me whether I could go, they changed the plans. They now needed me out there for the tennis camp in 10 days. They would sort of the visa, etc. I just had to get myself packed and ready.

It was chaotic and wonderful as I buzzed around London, saying goodbye to family and friends, getting everything together and moving all my stuff into storage.

When I stepped onto the Qantas flight, I was overjoyed at what lay ahead: a minimum of six months in the sun, starting with tennis camp. Can you imagine? What were they thinking - inviting me to a tennis camp full of fit young men? I was 23 when I went. I was young, ambitious and dying to have fun. And I was gorgeous - even though I do say so myself! When I look at photographs of me in tiny denim shorts, with long, blemish-free legs and a tight t-shirt that showed off my 34EE chest spectacularly well, I feel a pang of jealousy towards the younger me. The girl in the photo could get any man she wanted. The woman in the mirror can't!

I arrived in Canberra, the capital of Australia, after spending the night in Sydney and catching an internal flight early the next morning. I was told that I would be rooming with a woman called Fleur.

"Room 18. Head straight up," said the woman in reception.

I pushed open the door to our room and was pretty impressed with what I saw. It wasn't so much a room as a mini apartment with two large bedrooms, a small kitchen and a living area.

Sitting on the floor in the sitting room was a woman I assumed to be Fleur - this magnificent-looking woman with amazing Afro-style hair that created a huge bubble around her beautiful face. She looked up at me when I walked in.

"You must be my new roommate?" she squealed in a strong Australian accent, jumping up and rushing over boxes and bags to reach me. "My God - you are so sexy; everyone will want to bang you. I think I want to. Great tits!"

"Oh, right, Gosh. Thank you," I said.

"Oh wow. Amazing British accent, too. I think I might be in love with you."

"Well, that's a good start," I said, dropping my case and bag to the ground and exploring the apartment.

"I've saved the nicer room for you," shouted Fleur. "Since you've had a long journey. It seemed only fair."

"Oh, you're a star," I said. "I might go and lie down quickly now; I'm exhausted."

"No. Big mistake. You'll feel awful, won't be able to sleep tonight, and you'll be jet-lagged for a week. You must stay up today and go to bed early tonight."

"Really? But I did the long journey yesterday. I just did the internal transfer today."

"You've still got to stay up. It's the only way to do it."

"Christ, I'll be dead by this evening."

"No, you won't. Not if I take you out. Have you been to Canberra before?"

"I've never been to Australia before," I replied.

"Right - go and get yourself showered and changed and whatever else you want to do, and in half an hour, we're going out to meet my brother and his friends in Baterman's Bay."

"OK," I said. "I'll be as quick as I can."

I showered and slipped on a simple little white dress with spaghetti straps. I wore simple hoop earrings, left my newly washed hair loose and hanging down my back, and went to the sitting room to meet Fleur.

"Bloody hell, hot stuff. Come on, let's go. The men of Australia won't know what's hit them."

As we drove along, Fleur and I became more acquainted. She had been working at the Australian Institute of Sport (they call it the AIS, and it took me a while to realise what she was talking about) for some time and said it was great fun. She's from Canberra but worked in Sydney until she received a call asking her to join the AIS in Canberra.

"Are the people at the AIS good fun?" I asked.

"Yeah, most of them are. It's a huge place, and we

tend to stay in the medics' area, but there are some-times parties that everyone goes to - then you get to meet all the others."

I sat back in my seat and smiled. What an adventure this was going to be.

We arrived at Fleur's brother's house after almost two hours of driving, the second half of which I slept like a baby. When we exited the car, we were greeted by her brother Greg - a lovely guy - very Australian-looking with his tanned skin and blonde hair. He had those bits of rope tied around his wrists that lots of the surfer dudes seem to have. I looked at the ropey/stringy bracelets and saw how muscular his forearms were, with lots of blonde hair covering them.

I think he was younger than me and looked very wholesome and innocent but a little bit sexy.

We went inside, and his dog, Mabel, came bowling up to me, practically knocking me over.

"Be careful, Mabel," said Fleur. "She's fragile. She only just landed from Mud Island."

'You just got here today?" said Greg.

"Yesterday from London, I arrived in Canberra today. And what's all this talk about 'mud island'? Is that what you call our blessed country?"

"Yeah - it does rain a lot, and it is kind of muddy."

I shook my head. "The rain makes it green and beautiful, not muddy."

"It's green and beautiful here too. I'll take you for

a walk later and show you," said Greg. "How about we all go to Corrigan's Beach?"

"Sounds like a plan," said Fleur. "We'd better feed this young lady first, though."

Greg stood up. "Fancy a bit of breakfast?" he asked.

I wasn't sure what to expect for breakfast…I thought he would bring over loads of healthy food because everyone here seemed so fit and into health and exercise, but I was pleasantly surprised by the arrival of what looked like a full English breakfast.

"Wow, thank you. That's great," I said as we all sat down to eat. During breakfast, three of Greg's friends arrived and joined us.

I felt much more alert when I'd finished. I stretched my arms above my head and felt the tiny spaghetti straps pull tight. By the look on Greg's face and those of his friends, this displayed my breasts beneath the flimsy material to maximum effect. They all stared, making me stretch out even more.

"Come on, let's go and explore," said Fleur. "I want to feel the sand between my toes."

We walked along as a group, but Greg and I soon ended up adrift from the others, chatting amiably while Mabel danced around us.

"Come and sit here," he said, pointing to a bench with a fantastic view of the cliffs and the beach. I listened to the gentle hum of activity from the road and the sound of the waves. It was beautiful.

"I love this time of year," he said. "It's nice, but not too hot."

"Yeah - this is hot where I'm from," I said.

It was winter in the southern hemisphere, but still beautiful and sunny.

"Tell me if you get cold, and I'll warm you up," said Greg, giving me a mock cuddle.

I leaned him to him as he cuddled me and dropped my head onto his shoulder. His hand around me squeezed a little tighter, and I could feel him weaving his fingers in the thin straps of my dress. I wasn't sure how this had happened, but one minute, we'd been walking along talking about the Institute of Sport, and now we were all wrapped up on the bench.

His hand was still rubbing my shoulder and playing with my dress strap. I had small lace daisies sewn into the front of the dress.

"Do you like these?" I asked provocatively, pointing to them and knowing that if he looked down, my gaping dress would give him a view of my breasts.

"They are nice," he said, fingering the daisies.

I looked up at him, and we locked eyes; then he dropped his head and kissed me, his hands moving instantaneously to my breasts, which he massaged gently through the material of my dress. I could feel my nipples harden under his touch.

As he massaged more firmly, our tongues flicked

against each other, and I groaned. I pulled my head back from his kisses and looked around. No one was passing, so I pulled the straps of my dress down and sat there with my large breasts on show.

"You are very naughty," said Greg, sucking my nipples. I reached over and felt his large cock pushing against the fabric of his shorts. He had his hands all over my thighs as he bit my nipples and pushed his cock against my exploring hand.

I needed to feel him, so I gently unzipped and pushed my hand in to feel his hard cock. I rubbed him gently, and his hand moved to my thigh, roughly pushing his way up and easing his hands inside my panties. He stroked my clit with one hand while rubbing my tits.

"Oh God," I groaned, pushing myself into his hand. I could feel the heat rising inside me.

"You naughty pair!" said a voice.

We both looked up to see Harry, one of Greg's friends, standing there. "You have fucking amazing tits," he said.

I pulled up my dress, and Greg zipped away his erection.

"Please don't stop," said Harry. "I've got a hard-on just looking at those tits."

I looked down at the ground. I'd been so close to cumming, I couldn't bear it.

"Shall we head back to the apartment?" Greg said.

"Sure," I replied, standing up and following the two men.

I was desperate to feel his cock inside me.

THE SEXY AUSTRALIAN

*O*nce we got back to the apartment, it was a waiting game…waiting for a moment when Greg and I could sneak off. Fleur and Henry were there, along with Lee and Rich, all discussing setting up a garden barbecue. To be fair to Henry, he hadn't said anything to the others about finding us infla-grante´. The conversation had moved on to drinking and eating. There was only one thing I wanted him to eat - my pussy.

"Come on, we're playing softball," said Fleur, calling Greg and me over to her. As we walked over, Greg whispered to me: "Before you leave, I am making you cum."

"Thank God for that," I replied. "I've already taken my knickers off. I'm wearing nothing under this dress."

It was later, much later that we found ourselves able to escape. The hot passion I'd felt earlier had faded, but I knew the flames would be reignited as soon as he touched me.

He led me to the far side of the garden, where he laid out a blanket in the shade of a beautiful old tree. The others were all inside, watching television. I didn't know whether they realised we had sneaked off, but I didn't care too much. I was too excited about the prospect of what lay ahead.

I lay down on the blanket, and Greg lay next to me. I reached across and touched his jaw, my fingers barely brushing it, taking in the roughness of his slight stubble and the heat of his skin underneath. He groaned in appreciation as my fingers tangled in his soft blonde locks.

"Can I?" he asked softly, his arm sliding around my waist. As soon as I nodded, he pulled me close and kissed me.

That flicker came again, coursing through my body and settling below my waist. As his lips played over mine, his tongue sliding in, I moved closer, threading both hands in his hair and massaging his scalp.

"I feel like I'm in high school again," he murmured. "My hands won't stop shaking." He fumbled for the hem of my dress and pulled it over my head. I wriggled out of it. I was completely naked.

"You too," I said, watching him remove his clothes. He was staring at my breasts as he removed his clothes.

He lay down next to me, so we were skin to skin.

"Want a massage?" he asked.

I lay on my stomach and turned my head to the side as his fingers found their way to my neck, working out the kinks one by one, kneading my tense muscles.

"Too hard? Too soft?" he murmured.

"Just right, maybe a bit harder."

He straddled me to massage me more deeply.

With a knee around each of my hips, he started to work on my shoulders. Suddenly, his hands were all over me; I could hear him breathing. I was enjoying the massage and feeling quite relaxed, then suddenly, I felt a rush of excitement as his hands moved close to the sides of my breasts, and I needed him to have his hands all over me.

Without saying a word, I rolled over.

My hair was soaked with sweat; my skin was prickling; I wanted him to push my legs open roughly and force himself inside me. I didn't want any more tenderness. I know that sounds terrible, and, of course, I want to be treated well by men, but after a day of waiting for this moment, I wanted him inside me.

We kissed again, harder and faster and deeper, him groaning and me panting with desire.

As we kissed and touched, teasing each other with lips and fingers, his mouth travelled over my chest, sucking my nipples and letting one hand travel down to stroke my pussy.

"Fuck me," I said. I mean - I couldn't be clearer, could I? And he didn't need to be asked twice. He moved so he was inside me but carried on stroking me while he thrust himself deep into me. Soon, I heard a high-pitched sigh and realised it was coming from him.

We moved with and around one another, skin against skin, muscle on muscle; I gasped and closed my eyes before giving myself up to pure sensation. The throbbing between my legs intensified as I kissed and bit his neck.

"Yes, that's right, let it come, let it come," he said. Oh, God, it felt good. I stared straight into his lovely face as I came and came and wondered whether it would ever stop.

"You OK?" he asked when we had finished and lay in a sweaty mess.

"I'm great," I said, kissing him. "Are you?"

"Oh God, yes," he said. "We must do it again sometime."

"Yes, please," I said.

It wasn't until I was in the car travelling home later that I learned Greg was much younger than me. Whoops. I also didn't realise then that he was a brilliant rugby player, and around five years later, I saw that he was in the Australian squad.

Soon after that, he played in the World Cup. I wish I could tell you his name. Suffice it to say, he became very famous indeed.

HE PULLED MY HAIR AND BIT MY NECK

Fleur ribbed me A LOT for sleeping with her brother. At first, she couldn't believe I'd done it and asked me, 'But why, mate? What were you thinking?'

Then she opted for taking the mickey out of me on every possible occasion, even on the journey to work for my first day at the Australian Institute of Sports.

"Listen," she said, suddenly serious, as we approached the car park. "There are a lot of young people at the Institute - some as young as five. You must keep your hands off them, OK?"

"OK," I said. "I'll try my hardest."

I would be meeting Australia's leading tennis players who had returned to the Institute after Wimbledon and were resting and recuperating before starting all their training pre-Australian

Open. I was to be part of the squad that worked with the players in rehab.

The Institute was an impressive place; it was huge, and its grounds dominated the area. I knew it was incredible before I saw it with my own eyes, but I was shocked by the sheer scale of it when I did.

Fleur showed me through to the reception area of the tennis centre and made her way through to the field area. She was working with the Socceroos, who were based on the opposite side of the campus.

The receptionist introduced me to four players. One was famous at the time, and another of them is very, very famous now. The other two slipped through the net somewhere…like so many burgeoning internationals. All four were bloody gorgeous. I shook hands with them, dropping my head to one side and smiling coquettishly. I could never resist a little flirt back then.

The head of physio for the tennis section was a bouncy, smiley man who reminded me of an over-grown toddler with his enthusiasm for life. His name was Roger, and he greeted me like I was the mother he'd never met.

"My God. Hello, hello. Wow. You're here. That's great. So good to meet you. Come with me."

He was a portly man with a light brown beard that was all unkempt and seemed to go all around his neck and join up with his hair on either side of his head.

"I'd like you to get involved in Dan's recovery. Did you see Dan at Wimbledon? Tremendous player."

Dan's not his real name, but if I gave you his real name, you'd drop your cup of tea and make a dreadful mess of the carpet. He is PROPERLY famous. I mean - how many of the top-ranking male players do you know? He's one of them!

Dan had his own coaching team, physios and doctor and didn't need any assistance from me, but they were using the facilities at the AIS, which meant the AIS were involved, and part of the AIS's commitment was to 'provide qualified staff.'

Roger suggested that he show me around and introduce me to everyone then I should spend some time talking to Dan's medical team to find out ways in which I could help them.

At the end of the day, I met Fleur in reception, and we went for a drink.

"How did it go?" she asked.

"I met Dan," I told her. "He's fucking gorgeous. I spent the morning trying to work out how to get him into bed."

Fleur burst out laughing, sending wine splattering across the table.

"Aren't you supposed to be concentrating on his recovery?"

"That's exactly what I'm doing!" I said. In truth, I'd

done a lot of work with his team and had run through some techniques they said they would try. I knew they were impressed, so it was fine for me to fantasise a little.

"Will you be seeing him every day?" she asked.

"I'm not sure. There doesn't seem to be a clearly defined role for me, but Dan's people seem good and are happy for me to have as much input and as many ideas as possible. I enjoyed working with them."

"But you'd rather have been in bed with Dan."

"Well, yes, that's certainly true."

In the end, I did see Dan most days, and he made it pretty clear early on that he was attracted to me. His eyes would linger over my body, and he always watched me whenever I was in the room. He even winked at me once or twice, making my legs go to jelly. Nothing ever happened, though, because we were always with other people. I don't think I spent more than a minute with him alone.

Then, it was time for the tennis dinner.

"You must come," said Roger. "Dan is particularly keen for you to attend. You've been a great help to him."

"Thank you. I'd love to," I said.

The dinner was on a Friday night, and along with the invitation came a whole load of anxiety about exactly what I should wear.

I toyed with different looks in my mind. I couldn't go full-on seductive because it was an important work dinner. I contemplated going for a sundress with no panties for a look that screamed: "Good girl gone bad."

Too obvious.

In the end, I chose a light blue belted trench coat with strappy wedge-heeled shoes - sky-high but without the risk of toppling over that stiletto-heeled shoes brought. I didn't plan to remove the trench - a thin linen coat that looked like a wrap dress once it was on. It was getting chilly in the evenings, so that would work well.

In the three weeks I'd been in Australia, I'd noticed the winter coming in (not winter like we know winter in the UK, but a little bit colder than it had been when I first arrived). Underneath the trench, just in case it suddenly became very hot, I wore the tiny slip of a sundress I'd worn the day I ended up with Greg.

My hair was in loose curls that I ran my hands through, so they scattered all over my shoulders. Poor Dan didn't stand a chance in hell.

I arrived at the hotel restaurant and said hello to everyone. Dan leaned over and kissed me on my cheek. We'd been flirting for a couple of weeks, and he looked me up and down when I walked in.

"Anything underneath that coat?" he asked.

I smiled and gently shook my head.

"Really? Did you just say no?" he asked.

I winked at him and walked over to my seat.

To say that he stared at me throughout dinner would be an understatement…his eyes practically set my clothes on fire. I knew I had him.

After coffee, he came over to me and said goodnight. The players were leaving early to get a good night's sleep.

"Come to suite one," he whispered.

"Suite One. Of course - it had to be suite one."

"Just come," he said, passion burning beneath the words.

"OK," I replied as if he had persuaded me. As if I hadn't been thinking about this moment for weeks.

"Knock, knock," I said while gently tapping Dan's door. I straightened the hem of my trench and loosened the front. I wanted him to grab me as soon as he saw me. I don't know what that says about me. Perhaps I'm deeply insecure, but I wanted to see the look of lust in his eyes.

"Hi," he said, swinging the door open. "Do come in."

I walked into his amazingly sumptuous suite.

"Would you like a drink?" he asked.

To be frank, I didn't want to mess around with any preliminaries - I just wanted his cock inside me, hard and fast. I know that's shocking…but it's the truth. My nipples were hard, I was wet, and my body was thumping with need.

Dan was in the drinks area, pouring out two

drinks. I undid the coat and let it fall to the ground; then, I slipped off the tiny dress underneath. When he turned around, I was standing there completely naked.

"Holy fuck," he said, juggling the glasses before letting them both fall to the ground. He left the glasses on the floor and approached me slowly, staring as he walked. It was so exciting. Neither of us said a word.

He had his shirt sleeves rolled up, and the hair on his forearms looked thick and manly. My nipples stood out harder than ever.

"Well, this is all very lovely," he said, with his hands on his hips, looking me up and down.

I felt like such a slut. It was wonderful.

"I just popped in to say 'hi' and don't be late for rehab tomorrow," I said.

"Did you indeed," he said, rubbing his jaw. The sound of his hand against rough stubble was a real turn-on. I wanted him to touch me so badly that I almost grabbed his hands and put them on my body.

"You're making me hard," he said, just loud enough for me to hear.

I ran my hands through my hair, shaking it until it streamed over my shoulders and back.

"You're adorable," he said.

"Adorable is not what I was going for. I want you to want me. I want you to lust after me."

"Christ, woman, we've all been lusting after you

from the moment you walked into the AIS. You're all we talk about."

I knew he was probably making that up, but I didn't care.

I glanced down and could see the bulge in his trousers.

I could have cum on the spot, watching him watching me. Seeing the effect I was having.

Then he leaned in, held my head in his hands and kissed me tenderly. He didn't touch me, but the feeling of his clothes against my naked skin - rough and making me feel vulnerable - was a giant turn-on.

He pulled away slightly and removed his shirt. He was lean but incredibly muscular. He removed his trousers, too, gasping for breath as he did so. His boxer shorts came down, and his erection jumped out of his shorts…long and thinner than I expected.

"Bend over," he said. I left my shoes on and bent over the desk slowly. He licked and kissed down my back, making circles with his tongue on my bum cheeks, before his hands moved in and held my breasts, massaging them and squeezing my nipples as he entered me.

He started slowly, but I needed more.

"Harder," I breathed, and Dan obliged, beginning to thrust in earnest as my pussy widened, and I took it, over and over, his tongue on the soft skin of my neck a lovely contrast to the pounding.

"Ohhhhh fuck," I sighed, my voice high and deep at the same time. "Fuck, that feels good."

Curling my fingers against the edge of the desk, I moved my feet further apart to take him as deeply as he could go. I was rewarded straight away with a loud grunt behind me.

"That's right," he said as his balls hit my clit. I squealed with surprise and pleasure as he slapped me firmly.

"Slap me again," I said.

"Oh my God, you whore. Oh, you fucking whore."

I loved it when he talked dirty.

His hands travelled across my hips and up my stomach to pinch my nipples. He kept squeezing and pinching my nipples until they hurt, but in a sexy way. I started to see white-hot as he pumped furiously. I responded with a long, dramatic wail like I'd never heard myself make before, and he laughed.

"Are you OK there?"

"Oh God, yes. Fuck me harder," I said. He started moving faster, harder, deeper, fucking me as I'd never been fucked before, and then I started cumming, over and over and over again, as he licked my neck and pulled my hair so my head yanked back sharply and my back arched.

"Come on, you can give me one more," he said, fondling my breasts more vigorously. Then I felt it, another orgasm growing within me.

He pulled my hair harder and bit my neck as I screamed ecstatically, then collapsed on the floor.

He joined me, and we lay there, exhausted, flushed and drained.

"I loved that," he said.

"Christ, me too," I said.

"You have to go now. I have to sleep. But maybe we can do it again. Maybe I can tie you up next time?"

"Oh God, yes, please," I said, putting on my dress and coat and leaving. The next day at work, it was as if nothing had happened.

A NIGHT WITH THE
MUSCLE MAN

*a*fter six months in Australia, with summer in full swing, I decided to extend my stay for another six months, and I threw myself into trips to the beach for surfing, snorkelling, and swimming. I loved the Ozzy lifestyle. On the man front, I'd been very well-behaved since my filthy rendezvous with Dan, but there was someone I quite liked...the head of player protection.

A security team was attached to the famous players along with additional protection officers that the tennis stars employed privately. Then, a guy called Daryl was in charge of them all. He was called 'chief player safety officer' or something like that. He was large and gorgeous; honestly, he was all I could think about.

He had a huge reputation, having run the security teams at various Olympic Games, and he'd been in charge of player protection at the Australian Open and had taken on close bodyguard work for one of the players who had received death threats. The police were concerned that the threats were valid, so Daryl had been called to monitor things. Daryl was brave and muscular and used to work for the police in armed response. That's win, win, win in my book. This is probably a very primitive thing to say, but I LOVED the idea of a man with a gun protecting people.

Daryl and I had become friends and bumped into each other a fair bit, but he never seemed interested in me the way I was interested in him. I was getting frustrated that he only seemed to want friendship from me.

I decided to try my luck. "Hi, we're having some friends over for dinner on Saturday night if you fancy coming," I suggested. "Just a casual thing."

"Sure, that'll be good," he said in his strong Australian accent.

"OK, great. Is 7 pm OK?"

"I'll be there."

Now I just had to organise a dinner party.

I rang Fleur and told her what I'd just done, and she laughed a lot.

"OK, look, I'll invite a few mates over and see what happens," she said.

"Fab, you're a star," I replied.

She rang back about an hour later to say some of

her friends were coming, and she'd even summoned up the courage to ask a guy she liked.

"Perhaps we'll both get lucky," she said.

When Saturday night came around, I panicked about what on earth I would wear, what we would cook and how the whole thing would pan out. I even wondered whether I should go ahead with the whole thing at all, to be honest. I'd bumped into Daryl several times since asking him to dinner and checked that he was still coming. "Oh yes - thanks for reminding me. I'd forgotten all about that," he said.

What the hell! I'd thought of nothing else since inviting him; he had completely forgotten. Thanks very much!

I left it quite late to get ready, so I had little time to fuss. I just slipped on a pair of cut-off denim shorts, a crop top and a loose-fitting white shirt. I was tanned, which helped, and a healthy dose of lipstick helped even more. I hoped I looked under-stated but attractive.

As evening descended, I hovered by the front door, awaiting the arrival of 6-foot-7-inch, 20-stone Daryl. He was considerably over twice my weight and almost a foot and a half taller. There was something very sexy about that.

He arrived bang on time and looked gorgeous.

"Do you want something to drink?"

"Sure, a beer would be great," he said. "Then I want a tour of the apartment, please."

"It's not very big. That will only take five minutes," I said. We walked around - him looking at the place, me admiring how incredibly muscular he was. I noticed a couple of scars on his face that I hadn't seen before. This was a man who had been through some really bad stuff. There was an air of potential violence and fury about him. It was just simmering, and that made me both excited and anxious.

But there was no sign that he was interested in me. None. He mentioned a few security issues: we should have window locks, and the bedroom doors should have locks on them, but there were no longing stares or eager glances.

For dinner, Fleur and I prepared a chicken salad with avocado and walnuts, a great homemade dressing, bowls of gorgeous, crispy roast potatoes, and tons of garlic bread.

He ate silently, and I swear to God, I was on the verge of calling the whole thing off and just going to bed. Fleur's 'man friend' had his hand on her thigh under the table; Daryl was looking at the window frames and analysing whether they'd stop a speeding bullet. For God's sake - did the man never take a day off?

We moved through to the sitting room area while

Fleur and her man went to bed, and the others drifted off into the night. We put on a film, and I was so disillusioned with everything that I fell asleep on the sofa.

Hours later, I was awakened by a deep voice screaming from the armchair. *"Back off! Get back! Get off her, or I'll break you!"*

I jumped up. What the hell was going on? Was the house under attack? Then I saw Daryl, fists clenched as he lay slumped in the armchair, fast asleep. It must have been him shouting out. I wasn't sure what to do. Should I wake him?

I crept up to him and shook him gently. "Daryl? DARYL? Is everything OK? You were shouting."

"Aw, shit, that was a bad dream. Sorry." I could see that he was covered in sweat.

"Do you want a shower or something?" I asked.

"I don't want to impose."

Much to my surprise and growing delight, he seemed to look at me differently. He was staring at my breasts as I leaned over him. Perhaps tonight would work out OK after all.

Daryl headed for the bathroom, and I heard the shower running. Once it had finished, I took him a towel and threw it into the open door of the bathroom.

I heard him shout "Thank you" before he came out with the towel around him. His body was beautiful, scarred and beaten up, but all strong and manly.

Christ, he looked good. I don't think either of us knew what to do.

"I'm going to shower as well," I said, grabbing a towel and heading for the bathroom. I had no idea what would happen next…it all seemed so odd. We were dancing around one another, unsure what to do.

After my shower, I walked back into my bedroom feeling nervous. He was still standing in the room in his towel. I stood in front of him. What now? Why didn't he just make a move?

"You know, I was kind of scared when I first saw you," he said. "You are so gorgeous, and all the players fancied you. I didn't think you'd even notice me."

"I did notice you. I always stopped to talk to you."

"Yeah, I guess."

"I invited you here tonight."

"I thought you might want me to make up the numbers, or maybe you needed a bodyguard.

"No, I invited you because I liked you."

"Liked?"

"You're good company. I think you're nice. I like you. What's wrong with that? Why did you come?"

"Because you're gorgeous, and I fancy you like mad."

"Oh. Well, that's good."

And still, we stood there, just looking at one another.

"Kiss me, for God's sake," I said.

He laughed and kissed me. There was something so gloriously masculine about him - his hard muscles, rough face, the fact that he could kill a man by looking at him.

I stared into his eyes while I tore the towel from around his waist and moved my hands down to stroke his thighs. Then I wrapped my hand around his handsome, growing cock. He pulled my towel off me and watched me drop to the floor between his legs, letting my hair tease his lower body. I kissed him all over, pausing to take the head of his massive penis into my mouth and swirl my tongue around it. I licked and sucked until it grew hard in my mouth. He had his hand on the back of my head and was pushing me to go faster, but I didn't want him to cum. Not just yet. I wanted to have way more fun with him.

Instead, I jumped onto the bed and lay spread-eagled, inviting him to do whatever he wanted with me. He climbed on after me and took both my legs, pulling me towards him, so I slid along on my back. Then he licked up the inside of my leg, teasing, lapping, sucking on me. I could see the hard muscles of his arms and chest holding me down as he feasted on me. I writhed in his grasp, unable to get free while not wanting to. I wanted to be ravished, consumed, devoured. He continued licking, swirling and drinking me in, driving me to the edge of climax but stopping when I got close. "Oh, don't stop," I cried. "Let me cum. I want to cum."

Finally, he let me, flicking his tongue, circling his tongue and taking me right to the edge of climax before I fell in and surrendered myself to the beautiful feelings.

Then he lifted himself so he was kneeling in front of me - looking at me with my arms above my head, legs slightly apart, pussy glistening.

"Just fuck me, Daryl," I said as I spread my legs wide for him. "I want you to fuck me so much."

He lay on his back and pulled me on top.

He took his big cock and teased me - half entering me before taking it out. Playing, testing me, teasing me. Then he entered me. Christ, he was huge. I watched his face as I took in his cock and began to move, breasts bobbing as I fucked him. He played with my clit as I rode him and almost immediately came again. Then it was his time. His hips began thrusting faster, and then he came, crying out as his semen squirted into me.

After that, we lay beside one another, him stroking my hair as I stroked the scars on his chest, and then I traced down his body to his hips. As I stroked his thighs, I could see he had become semi-erect.

"What have we here?" I said, dropping down so my mouth was right beside his balls. "I think I have the perfect cure for that."

I wriggled myself around so I was lying between his legs and made a meal of his cock and balls. I licked and sucked and gently held his balls while my mouth went up and down on his cock. I kept my mouth on him, sucking and stroking. I loved the feeling that he was completely at my mercy. It didn't take long. "Oh God, I'm going to cum," he said before the hot, salty liquid shot into my mouth.

LEAVING AUSTRALIA WITH A BANG

My trip to Australia had been a real eye-opener. It had shown me that I had the confidence to get involved with the best sportsmen around (I mean in a professional sense, but - yes- in that sense as well), and I knew I'd made an impact (again - in a professional sense). I had learned from the people I'd met at the AIS and showed them how we did things in the UK. Now I had great references from some of the most impressive sports meds in the world and a contacts book full to brimming. Perfect. It had been a blast.

Fleur persuaded me to come to the bar with her for one last time before my flight home the next day. It was an unseasonably warm evening when we walked along the road that had become so familiar to me this past year.

"I'm going to miss you," I told my lovely friend. "Make sure you come to England soon. I'll look after you."

"Yeah, I will," she said. Then, in a much smaller voice: "I'm going to miss you, too."

As we walked towards the bar, I could hear the thump of the drums. It seemed much louder than usual...like a band was playing. It all looked very lively. I felt daft in my shorts and t-shirt; I should have dressed up more.

I unclipped my hair and gave it a little shake. I had a lipstick in my bag - I'd put that on once we got inside. I pushed open the door and was greeted immediately by the most tremendous cheer. Everywhere I looked were the people I'd got to know since I'd been in Australia.

"Oh, this is fab," I said, hugging Fleur. I knew instantly that she would have arranged this astonishing get-together. I looked around...there was Greg, Fleur's brother, whom I hadn't seen since the garden incident. I hugged him, then spotted Daryl and Dan next to him. I was so thrilled they'd come along to say goodbye, but it made me laugh that Fleur had unknowingly invited the three men I'd slept with while I'd been Down Under.

"What can I get you to drink," said Greg, walking me to the bar.

"A gin and tonic would be great, thanks," I said.

Dan came over and hugged me, saying how sorry

he was to see me go, and thanked me for all my help. Dylan told me that if I was ever worried about anything, let him know - he knew many people in England who would be happy to help me. "Big people," he said, lest there was any confusion. "People who will sort things for you."

Standing just in front of me was a man we'll call Rob. He was a tennis player and would become one of the best players in the world. He wasn't Australian and way too young for me, but I kept looking at him because he kept staring.

Eventually, I caught his gaze and smiled. He smiled back and came over to me. "I'm sorry you're leaving," he said. "I thought you were at the AIS permanently."

"No, sadly not."

They had offered to extend my trip again, but it was time to go home. If I stayed any longer, I'd get too used to the warm air, the active lifestyle, the beach and the hot men; I'd never go home! Greg arrived behind me and handed me my drink. "Do you know Greg?" I asked. "He's Fleur's brother."

"Oh hi, sorry, I don't think we've met," said Rob, shaking Greg's hand.

"You've been doing well," said Greg.

"Thanks, it's starting to come together," said Rob.

I left the two men to talk and wandered off to find Fleur.

My friend was nowhere to be seen, so I sat on a

bar stool, listening to the band and chatting with some of the medics I'd met while I'd been in Aus. Every time I looked around, Rob was staring at me.

After a couple of gin and tonics, I couldn't help myself... bringing my drink to my lips, I traced the tip of my tongue up the tiny black straw. Enclosing the top in my lips, I gently sucked. I looked at Rob the whole time I did it. It took him about five seconds to come over to me.

"You look very sexy when you're drinking," he said as if I was unaware of how provocative my little show was.

I smiled and winked (I never winked - what was I doing?). The band played, the drinks flowed, and I had a lovely time.

"Shall we dance?'

I pushed myself off the stool and began jigging my way over the small dance floor in the middle of the pub, just in front of the band.

My hips swayed subtly at first and then with bigger movements as the band moved onto a faster tune. Rob put his arms around my waist and pulled me close as we danced together.

As he spun me round, I watched him...his gaze moved from my ankles, up my calves and thighs, over my hips, and linger at my breasts. He bit his lower lip. I must be doing something right.

The song ended and the band announced they would take a break. The bartender played background music, and I returned to the bar to order another drink. I shuffled my feet in a kind of dance to the non-descript song playing over the speakers. I felt a hand slip down my back and rest at my waist. It was Rob.

"I'll get you another drink," he said, barging to the bar before asking me whether I wanted one. He had a glass of water while I downed another gin and tonic.

"Not drinking?"

"Christ, no," he said. "I'm getting competition ready. You should know that."

"Yes," I said. For a moment there, I completely forgot he was an international sportsman. He was just a man in a bar flirting with me while I was getting drunk.

"Shall we get some fresh air?" he asked.

"Yeah, good idea."

He led me outside, and as soon as we were a few paces away from the bar, he took my shoulders in his hands. "May I kiss you?" he asked.

"Um, OK."

He kissed me so gently...light, fluttery kisses. Most of the sportsmen I've been with have been assertive and domineering. In many ways, I find that quite a turn-on. But Rob was different. He was gentle and sweet and left me gasping for more.

"Is that OK?" he asked.

"Oh God, yes," I replied. "It's very OK."

He took a drink of his water, watching me as he

did. A drop escaped from the corner of his mouth and began to trickle down his chin. I caught the droplet with the tip of my index finger. His eyes tracked me as I brought my finger to my lips and licked the little droplet off.

"You are so hot," he said.

I could hear a noise behind us and turned to see a small group of people who had left the pub and were standing outside smoking.

"Come with me," he said. "I promise I'll bring you back here, but will you come with me for one minute."

"Where to?"

"The AIS," he said.

There was something quite exciting about the idea of going into one of the most illustrious sports complexes in the world with a huge sports star, with the sole intention of misbehaving.

I'd been so over-awed by the place when I first arrived that it felt wonderful to sneak in after hours.

"Do you have your entry card? I had to hand mine back."

"Yep - no problem," said Rob as we ran over the road and back into the complex.

We went inside and ran through the labyrinth of corridors until we arrived at the hall where they had set things up for the national judo squad. Today, the AIS has a separate Combat Centre, which is fully equipped and a great national training base for the country's leading martial arts exponents, but back then, things were a little more make-shift.

We ran into the hall and onto the soft judo mats. We were giggling like children, afraid to put the lights on and feeling naughty for having 'broken into' a place of work.

"What if they have cameras in here," I said.

"It's fine. NO cameras," he replied.

I wasn't sure but decided not to care. It was my last night here…I'd be in another country tomorrow. I pulled Rob towards me and kissed him. His arms wrapped around my waist, and his strong hands groped my backside, bringing me closer to him. I gently bit his lower lip. His eyes drifted closed, and he emitted a low moan of pleasure. I pushed my hands down his hips, caressing his denim-clad thighs before I brought them up to brush his growing bulge. At my touch, his grip on my hips tightened. He leaned in and grazed my earlobe with his lips. "I want you," he whispered.

He brushed my hair aside and kissed the hollow below my ear. Warm tingles bloomed from the spot. His hands drifted back to my hips, but that's not where I wanted them. I took his left in mine and ran it up my stomach and to my breasts. My fingers guiding his, he cupped and squeezed. My nipples pebbled and strained against my bra. I chaperoned his right hand down my outer thigh, over my dress. He nuzzled my head to the side and kissed down my neck. I reached down and lifted my dress. Could I be any more obvious? I was pulsing with want and anticipation. His fingers finally discovered skin and began to dance closer and closer.

Then, there was a sound, a movement at the door. We both stopped and lay still as we heard footsteps approach. His fingers were mere inches away from where I wanted them to be. Why did someone have to come in then, at that very moment? I could hear them pacing around by the door. This was horrible. I wanted to get up and scream at them to leave. Rob felt the same way. He wasn't waiting anymore. I felt his fingertips push aside my panties and begin circling my clit. I bit my lip to stifle the moan I wanted to give him. His fingers were calloused and warm. I began pushing myself into his fingers. I started to moan, aware that it was a mad idea and that whoever was at the door might come and find us. But then - to our joy - the sound of receding footsteps, a squeaky hinge opening, and a soft thud of the door settling back into its frame.

"That was close," I whispered breathlessly as his fervour returned. His fingers pressed and massaged my sensitive bud. Hot tingles emanated from between my legs and spread through my body. I pushed back into him. God, he felt good. He brushed his lips across my neck, his whiskers scratchy. With no warning, he slipped a finger deep into my pussy. This time, I couldn't stifle my moan as his thick, calloused finger pulsed in me. "You have no idea how much I want to bury my cock into you." His voice was husky, which made me wetter. He moved his hand away from my breast to hold me up around my middle as my legs weakened. I was getting close, but not fast enough.

While he finger fucked me, I massaged my clit. Spasms rippled through me. "I'm so close," I whimpered. In response, he pushed a second finger in and thrusted faster. My pussy clenched around him. The friction felt so good. I matched my pace with his. I moaned as the heat built to a crescendo and flooded over me, every muscle tensing. His arm tightened around me, holding me up as red-hot tingles ripped through me. He brought me down slowly, slowly pulling out from my swollen, tender sex. I leaned against him as he wrapped his arm across my chest and over my shoulder.

The bulge in his jeans pressed hard into my backside. Mmm, something to play with. Turning to face him, I pressed him against the wall. My hand cupped his bulge and gave him a gentle squeeze. A low growl rumbled in his throat. I unbuttoned his jeans and pulled down the zipper. I slipped my hand inside the opening and caressed him. He twitched under my fingers. I loved making a man twitch. His hands grabbed my still exposed ass cheeks and squeezed. I'd love to be riding him. My mind wandered as I imagined him between my thighs, his cock sliding deep into my pussy. His hands explored my bare backside, my hips, and the space between my breasts. My thoughts were cut short when all the lights suddenly came on. "Shit!" I begrudgingly retracted my hand from his fly.

This was a bloody nightmare.

"Wait here," said Rob, adjusting his clothing and zipping himself up. He walked to the doorway, and I heard him talking to whoever was loitering. The voices sounded angry, but I heard the door close and footsteps retreating. Rob was back beside me. He pulled off his clothes and mounted me. Not a word was spoken.

He pumped into me while I thrust my hips at him, and in a matter of minutes, he was crying out as he withdrew and spunked all over my stomach.

"Fuck, that was good," he said.

"It was really good," I agreed.

We lay back down on the mat.

"I've only wanted to do that for a year," said Rob.

"Well, you should have come and talked to me sooner," I replied. "Oh, and by the way - who was at the door earlier? The caretaker?"

"No, it was that great big lump of a security officer. Do you know him? Called Daryl. He was looking for you. I told him you weren't here."

I left the next day and didn't see my tennis hero again. As I mentioned earlier, he became one of the best tennis players in the world. I've seen him since, and he's always very friendly, but he operates in a different sphere now, surrounded by people and trailed by security staff (not Daryl, thank goodness!) When word seeped out into the international sports community that I was writing this book, there was a certain amount of concern, understandably. Players didn't want to be named. I assured those who called that I would not name them. When it came to Rob, he sent an email saying simply. "We had a nice time. I beg that you will not tell my name." Of course not, Rob.

TIME FOR A THREESOME

I returned from Australia after a detour around New Zealand, Fiji and Samoa, where I had a LOT OF FUN (read all about it in the next book). Then, I joined a small sports physiotherapy unit as their sports specialist.

Let's call the company 'Complete Physio.' I settled into life back home and began casually dating Paul, whom I had met in a pub near my home when I was out one night with Caroline. He was lovely, but I was away so much and not ready to settle down, and he had no desire to be exclusive either, so we just met up whenever we fancied it.

I was back living in a house with Caroline and another girl, Maria. The three of us were physios. Maria's boyfriend Simon was good friends with Paul,

71

so we made quite a group - out drinking and dancing together, and always trying to find a boyfriend for Caroline.

I was the only sports physio; the others weren't very keen on sports; they preferred working in rehab with people who'd suffered car crashes or had illnesses. Maria worked in the stroke department, helping sufferers regain as much movement as possible.

When it came to sports physiotherapy - I was obsessed. I'd always loved my job, but it had taken on a new level of importance since my experience working in Australia. I loved treating sportsmen and women; their injuries were fascinating...all so unique to their specialisms. A few years into the work, I could tell which sport someone did from the injuries they were carrying.

For example - how do you know if someone played netball at a high level? I'll tell you how - their knees are completely buggered.

It's the fact that you need to stop very suddenly when you catch the ball. You are not allowed to run with the ball, and the sudden stopping plays havoc with knees...particularly ACLs. A quarter of netball injuries involve the ACL.

There you go - you didn't expect that when you picked up this book, did you? You thought it would be non-stop sex, but instead, you're learning about netball injuries.

Now, then, let's get back to the sex…

The sports physio unit I worked for was based in London, which served a few local sports clubs and was also open to private patients, most of whom were leading sports people.

It was exactly what I wanted to do. I threw myself into learning as much as I could about sports and sports people. I went above and beyond in my treatment of them.

During my first month in the job at the new sports physio unit, I was given my client list for the day, and all the patients I was due to see that day were based at a well-known football club. The club was one physio down, so I was filling in. I jumped on the tube across London and arrived at the club with an hour to spare.

I introduced myself to the head physio, and he talked me through what was needed; then, I was given a list of players I'd be working with. I didn't recognise them initially, but one famous person was in the middle. I knew his name, and I knew of his reputation. If only I could tell you his name, you'd know exactly what I mean by 'reputation'. I admit I wasn't a fan of his, but I knew all about him and was excited to be working on a leading England player. Most of all, I was pleased they had trusted me to give him a post-training-session massage.

I got to the club and got everything ready.

The first few footballers I had to deal with were very young guys, nervous and quite fragile. They bought out motherly instincts in me as I massaged their skinny young bodies and saw all the bruises, scars and marks left by previous injuries. These boys were miles away from home, desperately hoping to make it onto the books of one of the biggest football clubs in the country. They must have realised that the chances of them ever playing in the first team were about a million to one.

Football clubs have a particularly reckless attitude towards young players. They are happy to sign players with talent before that talent has a chance to be realised, and if it never transpires - they are kicked out after doing nothing wrong. Clubs are happy to dump young players as fast as they sign them, leaving the boys' dreams shattered. Many young players have abandoned everything to try and make it in their chosen sport... everything, including family, friends, education, and work. It's a cruel sport, but ballet and theatre are cruel. Success is cruel because what you must do to get it is extraordinarily painful.

The very famous footballer was the fifth name on my list. He walked in, and I was surprised about how much presence he had. I know that fame itself brings a certain something, and people will stop and look when they see someone famous, but this was more than that. It was that star quality you sometimes get...when someone walks in, and all eyes swivel around. Some people exude a magnetism and stand out from the crowd. In the same way, a famous actor might steal a scene just by smiling; this man had "it."

"Hello, how are you doing?" I asked casually.

"All the better for seeing you," he said with a wink.

"That's very kind," I said, trying to be professional, but I did give him a little smile back in a way that hinted at mischief.

"Are you feeling okay? Any particular aches and pains?" I asked. I suspected he had no injuries or the main physios would be dealing with him. I imagine he just wanted to loosen up and get a massage to stretch his muscles after training. That was the case, so he stripped down to a tiny towel and lay on my massage bed. I began to work at his muscles, kneading them gently and commenting on any knots or muscular issues I spotted along the way.

"You're very good at this, aren't you?" he said, as I pointed out where I thought he'd had previous injuries.

"I've got a lot of experience," I said.

"I bet you have," he replied.

It was all banter at this stage. He was just a footballer confronted by a woman and could not do anything but flirt. I didn't think for a minute that he fancied me.

Then, the tone of the conversation became fruitier.

"Do you wear lingerie beneath that uniform?", "You are very beautiful", "I'd love to see you naked." The compliments came thick and fast.

I smiled at him, then gently licked my top lip. I was flattered that I turned him on and wanted him to take things further.

Then he touched my leg.

"Is that okay?" he asked.

"Yes," I replied, trying to carry on massaging him.

"Good," he said, pushing his hand up a little further until he touched the lace of my panties.

"Is that OK?" He turned his head to stare at me while slipping his fingers inside the lace.

"It's OK. It's all okay," I said, suddenly feeling wildly horny. He removed his hand and sat on the massage table; I could see the erection created under the small towel as he started to undo the buttons of my uniform. This was all happening so quickly. He was like some sort of sex ninja. He didn't kiss me; he just stared at me, his jaw set like he was concentrating with all his might.

"Come here," he said. "Let me look at you."

I stood there in my underwear. Luckily, it was the sort of sexy underwear you would want to be seen in rather than the scruffy stuff every woman keeps hidden away.

"Undo your bra slowly," he said.

I unclipped the back and let the bra fall to the floor, covering my breasts with my hands and titillating him before slowly moving them to reveal my nipples. Then I ran my hands all over them, licking my lips.

He sat up on the massage table and moved to come towards me.

"Stay there," I said, throwing my arms in the air and wriggling my hips.

The thought of him being this big sports star, adored by everyone and with every woman in his grasp, made me want to have him in my grasp for a few moments longer. He watched as I leaned forward and slowly removed my knickers, looking straight at him constantly, staring into his unblinking eyes.

"Climb onto me; get on top of me now; I need to be inside you," he said.

"No," I replied. I teased him and touched myself, turning around, bending over, and shaking my chest at him.

"Come here," he growled, jumping off the massage table and standing before me. He pulled me into him and kissed me.

"Get on me, on that table now," he said, winking at me.

He lay on the massage table, and I climbed on top, straddling him and holding his arms above his head.

"Do you surrender?"

"I surrendered when you walked in," he said.

I let go of his arms and wriggled my hips, pushing myself against him. He touched my breasts, sucked my nipples and kissed me passionately until I felt excitement grow.

"I want to be inside you," he said.

"That's a coincidence," I said provocatively. "Because that's exactly where I want you."

He lifted me and directed me onto him.

Oh, that felt good.

I could hear a slight noise outside the door, but I didn't care. All I cared about was riding this man until we both came.

Oh God, that's good, I said to him as he moved faster. I don't know what stage we were at when the door opened, and another player (equally famous) walked into the room, came over and stood right next to us, leaning his hand in to fondle my breasts.

I'd never been in a threesome before, but the feeling of one man inside me and another touching me was wonderful.

"Suck my nipples," I told him as if to confirm this was all alright. The man I was riding smiled and laughed.

"Good girl," he said. "You're a good girl."

The second player removed his clothes and began sucking my breasts urgently while I rode the player underneath me.

The second player then dropped his hand to my

clitoris and rubbed it while the first player moved his hands to my breasts. Oh God, it was wonderful.

I could feel hands all over me while I moved up and down on top of number one player. Hands were everywhere. I was lost in a daze of lust and excitement. I didn't know which hand was which.

As the fever mounted, and I felt myself coming towards orgasm, I took the cock of player number two in my hands, and he began to move backwards and forwards in the same rhythm as I was moving on the player beneath me. All three of us were sighing, groaning and moving together as one.

Then it happened: the orgasm cut through me. I had four hands on my breasts, squeezing so roughly but so sexily that I cried out.

It was like I was having two orgasms, one after the other. I pushed myself down onto the man beneath me, squeezing with all my might, arching my back and thrusting my breasts out as I cried in joy. As I came, I squeezed hard on the cock of the second player as he rocked himself into my hand.

"I want to fuck you, I want to fuck you," he shouted, but there was no way I was moving; I could feel player one stirring beneath me and pushing himself up into me. He began moaning, grabbed my hips and thrust himself further into me. Player number two pushed hard into my hand; as I felt him cum, I turned his cock so it faced me and let him cum all over my titties. The two men rubbed the cum into my erect nipples while I sat there, astride a man who would become one of the most famous footballers in the country.

ICE COLD NIPPLES

I never saw Paul again after the incident with the two footballers. We were never exclusive, so I didn't feel as if I was unfaithful or anything, but I was mortified with guilt. I might come over as a mad sex fiend on these pages, but I also have feelings - I promise you!

Paul was a good man, but while having three-somes with international football stars, I thought I should avoid any relationship with anyone - even a casual, non-committed one.

I didn't want to hurt him or anyone else. That's always been my view. If you're in a relationship, commit to it; if not, have fun.

People are quick to criticise me because some of the men I have slept with are married, but I think it's the person who made the commitment who's at fault. How is it my fault that a player stood up in church and promised all his friends and family that he would stay faithful to someone, then pestered me for sex?

As far as I am concerned, there is strict liability for extra-marital affairs - the person who is married and made a huge commitment to a partner is responsible for adhering to the promises. Not me. We seem to live in a world where everything is the woman's fault, regardless. I'm not interested in that twaddle. Don't get married if you want to have flings with busty, blonde physiotherapists. Before sleeping with you, I won't search your bedroom drawers for a wedding ring. You are the one who needs to be sure you're not hurting someone. It's your responsibility, NOT MINE.

I always took my responsibilities seriously. I knew I could not commit to Paul in any way, so I called it off. I was young and thrust into a world of gorgeous men when few other women worked in sports. The women working alongside me were being wooed by the players as much as I was, and they were enjoying it all as much as I was.

OK, lecture over!

One sport I knew very little about, but I did a lot of work in, was cricket. Believe it or not, there are lots of different aspects to it. It's a team sport, but it's an individual sport when the batter is out on the field, bat in hand, facing the bowler. You also have mini teams: the two batsmen at opposite ends, having to communicate with one another lest they cause the other to be run out, the fielders working together, and the captain on the field making sure that his decisions are the right ones.

Even within the art of bowling, you've got different types of players: fast bowlers and spin bowlers.

When I was learning about the sport and analysing tapes of players with over-use injuries, I became fascinated by all this.

The different types of players also have different types of injuries to contend with, so it can be a good sport to work in as a physio in terms of variety. Also, players tend to be quite bright and talk to you, and despite it being considered a boring sport by people who know nothing about it, it's full of interesting, funny people.

I don't know whether you've heard of sledging, but it's when fielding cricketers start verbally abusing the batsman as he's preparing to take his shot. For example, there was an incident when a bowler said to the batsman (trying to put him off), "Why are you so fat?" Quick as a cheetah, the batsman replied, "Because every time I sleep with your wife, she gives me a biscuit."

I like that sort of silliness and pettiness. It appeals to me a great deal. So, I was delighted to be asked to go along to one of the most famous county teams in the country to work with them for a couple of weeks on some serious shoulder injuries.

There was quite a complicated setup in England cricket back then, with the county and national sides at loggerheads over players. The county side had their medical team tending to players, but the national team physios were also involved. I was asked by the England team, for whom many of the players in the county squad played, to go in and check how serious the niggles and pains they were getting were; they also asked me to suggest rehab and treatment.

This meant that I had to work alongside the county side's regular physios to ensure these players – England stars – got the best treatment possible before a major international cricket match.

So off I went to the County Ground. I won't tell you which county team it was because the players I worked with were England hopefuls who became England stars. But it was quite a long way from where I was living then, so I was due to stay in a hotel for a week, go home for the weekend, come back on Monday and stay in the hotel for the second week. Over the weekend, in the middle, the players would be tended to by the county physios at the match they were playing.

That was the plan.

But in the end, I became so absorbed in the players' lives and getting them as fit as possible for England that I stayed for the weekend, travelling to the match with them and watching how they were playing to address how these injuries were occurring.

It meant I was away from home for two weeks, in a hotel with loads of cricketers. Oh, yes - you know where this is going now, right?

I arrived at the hotel, looking forward to helping the players all I could. I checked in and headed up to my room. I was just about to unpack my case when the county physios and the county doctor asked me whether I'd come to a meeting with them.

I headed down to the room the players called "the war room, " where all tactics were discussed. When I walked in, four middle-aged men were sitting there in their county blazers, arms folded, looking at me. They stood up en masse as I approached them and shook my hand so firmly that I immediately knew they weren't happy with my presence. They wanted to let me know who was in charge.

I hadn't thought about it before, but I guess they saw me as a threat…coming in from the outside - half their age and female (shock, horror!). Also, I was more senior - I was linked to the England team and had international experience. The players would undoubtedly listen to me rather than other physios because I was reporting back to the international manager, and he was the one they all wanted to impress. With the Ashes round the corner, getting into the England team was a huge priority for these men.

"I think we all need to talk calmly," said the team doctor. He was a portly man who didn't look like he had turned down too many pints or pork pies over the years.

"Sure," I replied.

"No one understands why you're here," he said.

"No one? The players and management are all aware." I said. "I've talked to many of the players."

"Right. Yes. Well, we manage the players. It might work well if you follow our lead and watch what we do. We can give you reports on how they are faring."

"No, I'll be working directly with the players. Is there anything else? I'm seeing Steve in 20 minutes."

"Steve? No one mentioned that. Why are you seeing him?"

"That's my job."

So few women were involved as physios back then that it was a shock for these men, and my presence was clearly emasculating.

I understood that, and I'd no need or desire to make them feel like I was stepping on their toes, but I had to do my job properly; that's what I was paid for.

"We do have this covered. There's no need for you to be here," the younger physio said.

"No one's doubting that; now I need to get ready. I look forward to seeing you later."

I left, and they looked from one to the other. There was no point in us debating things. I'd been told to do a job that should not undermine what they were doing, but I knew they would never see it like that, so the best thing I could do was leave.

Cricket's not like that anymore. It's a hugely sophisticated and professional organisation now. It was bloody chaos back then.

A little later, I went down to see Steve and examine a shoulder that had been operated on twice and was still giving him problems. I'd arranged for the England doctor to come down the next day to look at it, but I wanted to start immediately on any work I could do to encourage repair of the injured site.

He walked in after training and smiled at me.

"I've been hearing all about you," he said.

I had a momentary panic that he knew two foot-ballers, but it turned out that he was being kind - he knew of my reputation as an accomplished and experienced sports physio.

He showed me the mess on his shoulder where the two operation scars sat. He had a lack of range of movement, some pain and a considerable lack of power. The man was a bowler. Power through his arm was what kept him playing the international game.

"Have you been icing it?" I asked

"It's iced some of the time," he said. I knew he was lying. He wanted me to report that everything was OK, but it didn't look good when I started testing and feeling around the muscles.

"Look - you need to be icing it a lot, especially after training."

He looked at me blankly.

"Well, it's either that, or there's a chance you'll need another operation."

He dropped his head.

"We'll do as much as we can to get you fully fit and raring to go, and the way you can help us is to get on top of icing it regularly."

"Yeah, sure, doc. Will do," he said.

"Now, where is the ice kept here?"

Steve led me through a kitchen area where he got ice out of a small ice container. It was nowhere near enough for what was required. Barely enough for a large gin and tonic.

"Is this all that's here?"

"Yep."

Having ice baths is very common now; back then, it wasn't, but I knew from colleagues at the Australian Institute for Sport that ice baths greatly impacted recovery from injury. It was something that I encouraged all the athletes I worked with to do.

"I'll sort this out," I said. "We need your shoulder completely submerged, and it would do you a lot of good generally if we could get you having ice baths."

"Christ, that sounds awful," said Steve.

"You know - I'm not even going to try and tell you that it isn't, it's quite horrible, but if you want to extend your career and if you fancy being in the Ashes team - that's the way to do it."

"OK, deal," he said. "You get the ice, and I'll get into it."

I smiled at him.

"Now, let's check out the other shoulder."

A couple of days later, a huge chest freezer arrived, along with bags of ice. I switched the freezer on, offloaded the ice into it, and started to feel like we were running a much more professional organisation. I'd got hold of a barrel, which I planned to use to submerge the players, and as I filled it with water from a hose, I saw the team doctor and physios watching me incredulously. I don't know why...if they checked, they'd realise that cold water and ice have been used for centuries as a recovery tool. Blimey, didn't Napoleon's surgeon to the Grand Army use ice and snow? That was in the late 1840s, over 150 years ago.

Though the physios and doctor may have been shocked at my decision to install an ice fridge, the players weren't. Many of the other county sides had them, and those players who'd reached international level were well used to post-training freezing sessions.

I asked Steve to meet me down there after training.

"Oh God - I know what you want to do to me," he said.

I smiled. He had no idea what I wanted to do to him…

"I'm sorry, but it's into the ice chamber with your whole body. It'll make a huge difference to recovery."

"Are you going to come in with me?"

"No, I will stand here and ensure you spend enough time there."

"Shame. The prospect would be much more appealing if you were with me."

I looked up at him, and we did that 'locked eyes' thing when you end up just looking at one another as your heart beats a little faster and you feel out of breath. I felt flustered. He wasn't the type I'd usually go for, but I felt drawn to him.

He put his arm around my shoulder as if guiding me towards the icy water. "Are you not coming into this with me?"

"No," I said sternly.

"I promise to get in there if you come, just for 10 seconds."

"You just want me to remove my clothes," I said.

"Hell, yes," he replied, ripping his shirt off and chucking it onto the floor. There was something quite magnificent in the way he threw it. All I could think was how exciting it would be if he ripped off my clothes like that and forced me into the ice with him. But you'll be pleased to hear that I pulled myself back together and looked at him.

"I'm not going in, but you are. Stop wasting time."

He was staring down at me, smiling that seductive smile of his.

"I'll take my shorts off, shall I?" he said.

"Yes, would you like me to go out?"

"That's fine," he replied. Under his shorts, he wore Speedos. He leaned over to feel the temperature and flicked the icy water onto me.

"Boy, that's bloody freezing," I said.

"I know it is, and you want me to get in there."

"It'll be very good for you."

"I think you should come in as well, just to show me what to do."

"I'm not going in there," I said, stepping backwards as I smiled at him. He flicked water at me again; it landed on my neck and chest.

"Sorry, I couldn't resist that," he said. He walked over to me and wiped away the droplets of water that had settled on the top of my cleavage. I murmured my approval; it was all he needed.

"Did that feel nice?" he asked.

I looked at him. I knew I should say, "No, it didn't. Stop wasting time and get in the water."

I didn't say that; I smiled at him and said "yes" in

my most seductive voice. That's when he kissed me so hard that it made me step back.

"I fancied you the first time I saw you," he said.

HE KISSED me again and slowly caressed my body, stroking my already-aching breasts. He undid the buttons on my shirt and moved down to kiss the lace covering my nipples. I buried my fingers in his hair as he eased his tongue under the lace to find my nipple. Then he held my hands up while his tongue continued teasing my breasts.

"This has to come off," he said, pulling my shirt, undoing my bra, and throwing them both to the ground. He made me keep my hands in the air as his tongue circled my nipples.

It felt wonderful. Then he reached into the barrel, took handfuls of ice, and rubbed it over my breasts, forcing my nipples to go rock-hard.

He kissed my breasts again, pulled down my trousers and panties, and lifted me onto the chair. He began to tease my pussy with his tongue, licking and sucking, slipping his tongue in and out as I pushed my legs further apart.

I was worried about coming too soon, so I moved his head up and made him kiss me so I could taste myself on his lips. I pulled down his speedos over his cock, stood up and pushed him down into the chair, dropping my head into his lap and running my tongue up and down the shaft of his cock as he groaned. I dropped my mouth over to the end of it and sucked gently, holding the base firmly with my hand. I pushed my lips close together as I sucked in and out, moving my tongue around on the shaft of his penis to give him an extra thrill. "God, Oh God," he said. I felt a salty taste; I knew he wasn't far off coming. I was still desperate with anticipation and longed to have him inside me.

"Come here," he said, so I clambered onto the chair, straddled him, and let him push himself inside me. I jigged up and down, allowing my breasts to dance in front of his face, my nipples still rigid. I ran my hands through my hair, then rode faster, moaning and wriggling atop him.

"Fuck, you're sexy," he kept saying. "You are so fucking sexy."

I groaned in delight as I felt the fires rise inside me. Then he groaned too - louder and lower, like a wild animal.

'Fuck, this feels good. Oh, it's so good."

We fucked faster and stared at each other as our orgasms mounted, and we collapsed on top of one another with cries of joy.

"Oh, that was good," I said. "And now I get to watch you in the ice bath and feel horny all over again."

He kissed me lightly on the top of my head. "And then we could do it again?" he suggested.

We didn't, sadly. Knocks on the door and other players arriving put a halt to any further fun. But I got to know Steve well during my time with the county side. We exchanged kisses and quick fondles after that, but nothing like that first time.

He has remained a friend over the years, and even recently, I've helped him out with an injury, and we both joked: "Not like when I was a player, is it?"

After I'd worked with him for those two weeks, he got back into the England side and made it into the Ashes team.

He was interviewed by a cricket journalist and said: "Yes - thanks to my wonderful physio, I'm fully fit and raring to go." He named me in the piece, which pleased me because I knew how much it would annoy the county physios, who resented me.

SHAG BADGES ON TOUR

Soon after finishing my short stint in county cricket, I returned to the clinic and resumed regular work with patients. Then, I got an email out of the blue from the secretary of the county side. She said that a guy had phoned in, wanting to speak to me; his name was Richard Hall, and did I want to speak to him? She had his number if I did.

I took the number and called him, hoping it was the Richard Hall I'd known many years ago when I was on the post-grad sports physio course. He was one of the lecturers, and I'd been quite close to him (not like that!).

It turned out that when the cricketer had mentioned me in the paper, Rich saw my name and tracked me down to the club.

"Hello, stranger," I said, hearing Richard's familiar Somerset drawl when he answered the phone.

"Well, if it isn't my favourite student. Fancy dinner one night?"

We made a plan to get together the following Thursday. We had to meet late because I saw a patient at 7 p.m. I didn't have time to go home and change, so I looked in a complete state when I got there.

"They are working you too hard," said Richard after I'd crawled through the door.

"No - they're fine. I'm working myself too hard."

He'd already ordered a bottle of wine, so I took a large gulp and sat back.

Richard explained that he was still working at the university and was now running the graduate course.

"Don't you miss the actual work, though? You know - all the hands-on stuff...seeing all the improvements in the broken bodies."

"Yeah, I do. And I take on projects occasionally, but sports stars are monsters. I think I have too delicate a disposition to deal with them."

I laughed so much that I spurted my wine out across the table. "You? Delicate?"

"I think I am," he said.

He explained that he had been the consultant physio on a major rugby tour a few years ago, and what he'd witnessed had shocked him.

"Really? I love the idea of working with a touring side - trying to keep them together so they can play all the way through without missing any matches."

"Yes - it's good fun and certainly challenging. Tough, though. I'm not sure those places are for women."

"Oh, OK, Mr Sexist. So, I'm not allowed to go on rugby tours, am I?"

"No, I don't mean that. Of course, you must go if it's something you want to do, but I was shocked about what these guys were like when they were away from friends and families for a month. And not just the players - they all acted like animals."

"Oh, do tell," I said, topping up our glasses. The more he drank, the more he was likely to reveal to me the quiet goings behind the scenes on tours.

"OK. Let's start with the badges."

"Badges?"

"Yes - they had a load of little metal pin badges made to hand out to children who came to watch the squad in training. They had the symbol of the tour printed on them. It was all part of their commitment to the country they were touring…they did training sessions and 'come and meet the players' sessions and gave out signed balls and posters and all these little badges."

"That's nice," I said. It didn't seem very controversial.

"The players kept hold of some of the badges and called them shag badges. They would give a woman a shag badge when they slept with her. But only the first time they slept with her. You couldn't give her more than one. Then you'd see a woman walking around the hotel the next day, proudly sporting a badge, and you'd think, 'yep - one of them shagged her.'"

"That's horrible. But the way you tell it, it sounds like the players were using the women. Perhaps the women were using the players just as much."

"I'm sure. Look - you can't get all feminist about it. I'm telling you all this from the players' point of view - it was their game - they were giving out the badges."

"It was their 'game'?"

"Yes - because what they were trying to do - and you're not going to like this, but it's true - they were trying to all sleep with the same woman, so she had loads of shag badges. Then they'd all laugh heartily at the woman walking around with a chest full of badges. They were only allowed to give out a badge the first time they slept with a woman, so if a woman had more than one badge, she'd slept with more than one player."

I shook my head as if disgusted, but I could quite imagine why these women were sleeping with all the players. I mean – come on – have you seen the bodies on rugby players?

"More gossip…" I said excitedly.

"OK, there were a few incidents with prostitutes."

"Yes, tell me all."

"A well-known rugby journalist went to see a

prostitute, and as soon as they were alone together, the prostitute beat him up and stole his wallet. Turned out it was a man in drag."

"Oh Christ, you don't expect that from a journalist. You'd think they would be too busy looking for players doing naughty things, not doing naughty things themselves."

"You'd be surprised," said Richard, taking a large gulp of wine. "All the men on these tours just lose their minds."

"Yeah – I guess it's the whole 'what goes on tour, stays on tour' mentality."

"There's another story, but it's so shocking I don't want to tell you."

"For God's sake, tell me," I said. "I promise not to be shocked."

"Well, you know how there are sponsors on every tour...like kit and travel sponsors, and overall sponsors, ball sponsors, and sponsors of the TV coverage. Christ, the sport is awash with sponsors.

"Well, one night, the team of four guys from the kit sponsors decided they wanted to have some fun, so they hired a prostitute for the evening, and one of them had sex with her while the others all stood around the edge watching them and wanking."

"Holy fuck, that's disgusting," I said. "Why didn't they just get prostitutes of their own?"

"I don't know. That's a perfectly reasonable question. I don't know why anyone would want to watch his mate having sex with a prostitute while wanking in front of the rest of his mates. It's hideous; that's why I didn't want to tell you."

"Yeah, that's pretty rank, I'll give you that."

"I don't think there was one player who stayed faithful to his wife or girlfriend. Not one. You're right - the whole 'what goes on tour, stays on tour' thing makes everyone believe they can do what they want…like there are no rules of decency.

The place was heaving with women, and the players were sleeping with them all while coaches, kit men, journalists, and other guys hoovered up the remains."

"But players are a bit like that, anyway, aren't they?" I said. "I mean - they're a fairly over-sexed bunch."

"Yeah, but it's all worse on tour. Promise me you won't go on a tour…"

"I promise," I said.

I broke that promise. The next book tells all the intimate details in all their colourful glory!

STORY TIME

I want to tell you about a famous and talented professional striker named Marcus Cooper. Marcus was known for his lightning-fast speed and impeccable ball control, making him a valuable asset for any club. However, fate had a different plan when Marcus suffered a devastating injury during a crucial match.

Marcus made a daring run down the left wing on a cold winter's afternoon. With a sudden change in direction, his right foot caught the turf awkwardly, causing his ankle to twist violently. A sharp pain shot through his leg. The stadium fell into an eerie silence as Marcus clutched his injured ankle, fearing the worst.

Recognising the severity of the injury, Marcus's team promptly arranged for him to see one of the best sports physiotherapists in London.

Known for her expertise in sports injuries and her experience in treating some of the world's best athletes, this wonderful physio successfully rehabilitated many athletes, helping them return to peak performance.

With hope in his heart, Marcus arrived at the physio's clinic to be greeted by her friendly and compassionate team.

The physio delivered the diagnosis after a thorough examination, including assessing his range of motion and stability. Marcus had suffered a severe ankle sprain with potential ligament damage. The news weighed heavily on him, knowing that recovering from such an injury could be long and challenging.

To initiate the treatment, the physio emphasised the importance of immediate rest and ice application to reduce swelling. She prescribed anti-inflammatory medications to alleviate pain and accelerate the healing process.

As Marcus progressed through the initial recovery phase, targeted physical therapy exercises were added to his treatment plan. These exercises aimed to improve stability and range of motion and strengthen the muscles surrounding the ankle joint. Marcus dedicated himself to the prescribed exercises, attending regular physiotherapy sessions and diligently following the physio's instructions.

Weeks turned into months as Marcus's determination and the physio's expert guidance gradually yielded results. With each passing day, Marcus regained strength and stability in his ankle and slowly transitioned from basic exercises to more demanding activities.

Finally, after several months of dedicated effort, Marcus received the news he had longed for - he could start training with the team again. The joy and relief that flooded Marcus' heart were indescribable.

With renewed determination, Marcus rejoined his teammates on the pitch. Although he knew he had to rebuild his fitness and regain his form gradually, he embraced the opportunity with gratitude and enthusiasm.

He also offered gratitude and enthusiasm to his physiotherapist, who had helped him so much in his recovery. He took her out to dinner to say thank you.

They got on very well over dinner, and Marcus said, 'Hey - why don't you come back to mine for a glass of champagne?'

"OK," said the physio.

And they headed back to the man's house. The physio smiled to herself at how luxurious the apartment was. It was incredible, and she knew he also had another big house near his club. This was just his London retreat.

"Come here," said Marcus, pulling the woman towards him and holding her tightly. "Stay the night..." The woman wanted to stay the night but wasn't sure whether that was a good idea. This was a very famous footballer, and she was worried that photographers might see her leaving. This man was always in the papers; she didn't want to push her luck.

Then he kissed her.

And it was lovely.

And he kissed her again.

Now, she was all hot and bothered. It was too late. She was staying the night.

First, though, the physio would tantalise the famous footballer a little...she liked to do that. She began to undress about a metre away from him. The footballer smiled and stroked his lightly bearded chin. He sat down in the big, comfy armchair in the perfect, tidy apartment, and the physio let her little dress fall down her arms and legs, revealing black lingerie and black stockings.

The footballer had his fingers entwined and his arms behind his head as he watched her closely. She unclipped her bra, and the footballer couldn't wait any longer. He stood up, grabbed the physio's hips and pulled her into him. He began playing with her breasts, his hands holding them as if they might run away. Then he slowly pulled down her panties. When they reached the floor, she moved one step closer to him, in silence. Gently, he kissed down the length of her body, kissed her tummy and turned her around to cover her back with kisses while letting his hand fondle her breasts. Then he took her hand and led her into the bedroom, where he threw her on the bed, climbed on top and slipped his hand between her legs.

His fingers gently slid inside her. The Physio closed her eyes and moaned while his right hand gently caressed her nipples. Then the footballer made her lie back while he kissed her breasts. His teeth closed in on the physio's nipples, his tongue circling to make her react. The physio groaned, then she pushed the player's head downwards, admiring his many tattoos as he traced down her body with his tongue, nibbling and circling as he went. He was such a good lover that the poor physio could hardly breathe for excitement.

She opened her legs wide. The footballer kissed up her thighs, guiding his head so his tongue lapped away at her.

She was completely at the mercy of the footballer and his licks and bites. Then, the woman's body arched.

"Stop," she said.

"Why?" said the footballer. "I want you to cum."

"I don't want this to be over too fast," said the physio, writhing beneath the tongue of the ardent footballer.

But it was all too late. The physio felt the heat rise, and an orgasm consumed her. She lay on the bed, arching her hips towards the footballer's mouth, eventually crying out before collapsing.

"How was that?" asked the physio.

"Wonderful," said the footballer. And that's how the physiotherapist slept with a very, very, very famous footballer.

I'M A BIT TIED UP AT THE MOMENT

*O*nly one word could describe this man... gorgeous. He was about 6'3" tall and had deep olive skin, chestnut, brown hair, and dancing green eyes (slightly altered description to protect the identity of the innocent). He was about the sexiest man I'd ever seen. But even though he was very handsome, he had such a dismissive attitude that I wasn't taken with him. He even treated his coach with contempt; in return, it was as if his coach despised him.

This man – let's call him Joe – stood apart from the other athletes. He didn't join in with them, didn't train with them, and didn't seem to be liked by them. I was quite baffled by him.

I'd come to see him because he needed my help. He had an ongoing Achilles tendon injury that had been operated on but still gave him a lot of pain.

There was also an impact on his range of movement: a disaster for an international athlete. I'd weighed the whole thing up with a biomechanist and devised a solution, which involved me trying to get much more flexibility around his hip joint.

This had been relayed to his coach, who invited me down to meet him. I had put a lot of work into this, and I thought Joe would be delighted.

But when I introduced myself to the athlete, I was met with no response at all. He just shrugged and walked away.

I went off to see his coach, whom I'd spoken to on the phone and had advised me to come down. I arrived at his office and knocked on the door gently.

"Come in," he shouted. I walked in to find him standing there with his hands behind his back, looking out onto the vast fields around his office.

"I don't know whether it is a good time, but I'm the physiotherapist. I wanted to introduce myself before we start work with Joe."

He spun round. He was much more handsome and younger than I would ever have imagined. Something about the word "coach" immediately makes you think of a grizzly 50-year-old in a horrible nylon tracksuit. He wore a shirt and trousers and had a lovely face and great hair. He wasn't an absolute beauty like his Joe, but he had a warm smile and a gentle disposition that his charge desperately lacked.

"My goodness – you're much younger than I thought you'd be," he said.

"I take lots of drugs," I said jokingly. "One of the benefits of working in medicine...great drug access."

He laughed and invited me to sit down. As I did, I could feel his eyes travelling up and down my body and lingering around my chest, where the tightness of my shirt gave him every idea about the size of my breasts. I almost wanted to say, "My eyes are up here," but I was getting quite a buzz from how he stared at me that I found myself arching my back a little just to make sure they stood out.

"Shall we discuss Joe?" I said. His eyes met mine, and I smiled at him as if to say, "I know where you were looking."

"Sure, of course," he said. "Do you fancy a drink while we talk?" He pulled a bottle of champagne from his desk drawer and handed me a glass.

"Oh, thank you," I said.

"It was a gift. I was set a dozen bottles," he said, clinking my glass with his. "I don't usually have champagne on hand."

I laughed, and he got back to the serious business of his athlete.

"Listen, Joe's tricky. He's got a complicated home life and had some tough things happen. He had bad news this morning; it's not a good time to talk to him."

"Why didn't you tell me before I came down here?"

"I thought it would be good if we talked, and you ran through everything with me."

"Did you receive the report from the doctor and the biomechanic?"

"Yes," he said, pulling some notes from his bag and plonking them before me. He'd made some hand-written marks on them, which I glanced through.

"If you could answer any of those questions, that would be very handy."

I started reading through his queries...he wanted to know how long various procedures would take and when his star runner could return to competing. I answered his questions, and as I read on, he lifted his chair to my side of the desk and sat beside me, reading the document simultaneously. It was most disconcerting. All I could think about was the feel of his leg resting against mine. He was so close to me that I could feel his breath on my neck. He touched my arm lightly as he went to make a point. He did it in a friendly way, but it was kind of distracting as I endeavoured to explain the finer points of ankle anatomy to him.

We continued in that vein for a little while until we had been through all his queries.

"That's great. You've been so helpful," he said. "Fancy an early dinner before you leave?"

"Sure, that would be nice."

We walked outside, where a car waited for us to sweep us away from the track. I relaxed into the back seat but could feel his eyes on me the whole time. I couldn't help but tease him a little as I crossed and uncrossed my legs, catching his eye as I did so.

He looked flustered, and I felt flustered.

It seemed a shame that we would spend the next few hours in a restaurant.

"Just here's great," he said to the driver, jumping out and opening the door for me.

We had pulled up outside a lovely glass-fronted house.

"Is this a restaurant?" I asked.

"It's my house. I was going to cook for you."

"Oh. OK."

I knew what that meant, and excitement rose inside me. I could see how he was staring intently at me, his eyes lingering on my waist, legs, and chest.

We went inside, where he poured me a glass of champagne and led me to the sofa.

"I find you very attractive," he said, removing the glass from my hand and placing it on the table.

"I find you very attractive," I replied.

Then he kissed me with an urgency that made me moan out loud, running his hands down my body and pulling me close. Every bit of him felt hard and strong.

"Do you want to have some fun?" he asked.

"Yes," I said quietly.

"I mean – some real fun."

"Yes," I repeated.

He reached behind him for a long ribbon. It was scarlet and looked like the ribbons they use in rhythmic gymnastics.

"I'm going to tie you up," he said.

"Oh God," I muttered. I loved the feeling of being tied up. I don't know why…perhaps the vulnerability you feel or how he's in total control. The feeling was extremely sexy.

"What are your fantasies?" he said, "I want to know your greatest desires."

"This," I said, "I like this."

Biting down on my lip, I stared at him as he held my hands above my head and ran the other hand down to my breasts to feel my hardened nipples pushing up through my dress. He reached over to undo the zip, which went from the top to the hem. He stared at me the whole time. I wasn't wearing a bra and only a tiny pair of lacy knickers, which he removed with one quick pull. Then, he led me to the bedroom, held my hands up, and tied them to the bedpost. I lay there, naked and exposed, with my hands tied above my head, and it felt so damn horny I couldn't stop myself from wriggling around. Lying there, feeling naked and exposed with him fully dressed, was so sexy.

He removed his shirt, and I felt another wave of

desire as I stared at his tanned, muscular chest, hard above his bulging trousers.

He leaned down and kissed me, his lightly stubbled cheek brushing against me. Then he licked down my body and sucked my left nipple. He took the right nipple and rubbed it under his thumb as he bit down teasingly.

I groaned with desire when he slipped his fingers inside me, and I pushed and wriggled against his hand. I felt myself opening up to welcome him in, lost in desire, as he stroked my clit with his thumb. I could feel my arms being restrained, my breasts being fondled, and my pussy finger fucked. When I climaxed with a small cry, he took his hand away and kissed me.

The sight of him fighting to restrain himself, still dressed from the chest down, while I was naked, ready, and waiting was a massive turn-on. Every time I wriggled or arched my back or moaned, I'd see this flicker in his jaw, which reminded me that he must be bursting to fuck me.

He worked his way back down my chest with his tongue, flicking my nipples and kissing them before reaching my sex. He began stroking, kissing, and licking while his hands gripped my legs, and I writhed underneath him, gasping in pleasure.

I can't tell how long this lasted; I never wanted it

to stop. Eventually, I begged him to fuck me. I needed to feel him inside me.

He tore his trousers off and entered me, and I lost all sensation other than the awareness of him filling me and touching me in places that felt as though they'd never been touched before.

We climaxed together, and he fell onto me, sweaty and panting.

"How was that?" he asked, undoing the ribbon.

"I loved it," I told him. "Absolutely loved it."

"Good," he said, winking at me.

We lay there for a while, chatting and working out which people we both knew and talking about great sports moments and great sports people.

Then I looked at him and let my eyes travel slowly down his body.

"It's your turn now," I said, reaching for the ribbon and tying his wrists to the bed.

I took him in my mouth and ran my hands over his chest as I sucked and licked, feeling more aroused with each of his groans.

He was thrusting up as I sucked on his cock, urging me to mount him, but he couldn't move me on top of him because he was tied tightly to the bed. Then I began to feel he was on the brink of cuming, so I climbed on top of him and began rocking back and forth as he filled me.

Then, in one swift move, he broke his hands-free of the ribbon and moved them to my hips, where he moved me more quickly backwards and forwards and began cupping my breasts and groaning. The roughness of how he'd pulled out of his restraints and his sudden urgency made me feel even more turned on. He ran his hands down onto my waist and moved me up and down. As soon as I began to climax, he rolled me over and held my hands over my head again as he pushed himself into me, thrusting wildly until he called out my name.

"Fuck, you're gorgeous," he said. "Absolutely fucking gorgeous."

HANGING AROUND BARS

*D*o you have any idea how fit gymnasts are? How brave they are, and how resilient? I worked with a group of gymnasts in pre-Olympics and was astounded by them. Any textbook will tell you that they are among the fittest of sports-people. Still, when you see them in action...when you see how they display strength, agility and both aerobic and anaerobic endurance, you see what unique specimens they are. And male gymnasts are gorgeous - like action men - all firm, toned, and bulging out everywhere. Watch a male gymnast do a crucifix on the rings (where they hold themselves - arms fully outstretched). Jesus Christ.

Anyway - I was working with a mixed group - the tiny female gymnasts throwing themselves upside down and inside out and doing 100 press-ups before going home, and the muscular men grimacing their way through mind-bendingly tough routines. I know most people prefer women's gymnastics - the routines are better choreographed, and they have a stronger performative edge than the men's sport. Still, I grew to prefer the men's sport because it challenges every bit of the body in every way.

I'll explain as we go through this, but it's a truly magnificent sport.

It's a gift for a physio because they get injuries all over. I mean - truly - from fingers to toes. And the injuries the guys present with are quite unpredictable. Because the whole body is involved, it's not like, say, tennis, where you're expecting injuries to occur in joints, or netball, where it's knees a lot of the time - there are injuries all over the body, and the injuries vary enormously from breaks to internal organs being crushed, stress injuries, collision injuries - you name it - they have it.

The sport requires strength, power, agility, and exceptional body control, meaning the bodies are compact and well-proportioned, unlike some sports where athletes can end up with extraordinarily large shoulders or particularly huge legs.

I went out to the Rio Olympics (not with Team GB, but with another country) and spent a lot of time in the athletes' village (more of that in my next book, all about sex with Olympic athletes). You'd think that the place would be home to the fittest people on the planet, but - instead - it's like a freak show. A group will walk past, all 7' tall, and then the massive weight lifters, wrestlers and heavy-weight boxers will lumber into view, weighing up to 27 stone. The gymnasts aren't freaky - they are small, but they are so well-formed. And - trust me - I know!

A particular gymnast whom I was asked to work with had muscles on muscles on his shoulders, as well as a defined, muscular chest.

I was told to look closely at his shoulder muscles (deltoids), biceps, triceps, and chest (pectoral muscles).

"OK, no problem," I said.

There was no particular injury worry about this gymnast other than coaches were concerned about his flexibility after putting on a lot of muscle. They wanted him to be in the best shape of his life for the Games and wanted to predict any problems arising before they happened.

Flexibility is vital for gymnasts as it allows them to achieve the extreme positions required by certain routines and skills. Male gymnasts often possess excellent flexibility, particularly in their shoulders, hip flexors, hamstrings, and back.

This flexibility enables them to perform intricate movements, maintain proper body alignment, and prevents them from getting many ligament strains and muscle pulls that other athletes get. This is important because they push their bodies to such extremes of flexibility that it can be serious when they get injured.

When you couple this with how short their careers are, it's vital to stay on top of all the preparation they need before competing and respond to all the injuries with lightning speed.

I went to Lilleshall, the national training centre for many Olympic sports, including gymnastics. I wandered into the huge gym and met with the other physios there. I recognised a couple of them. When I returned from the AIS, I'd given a talk, and a couple of these physios had come along to listen to my words of wisdom.

I was immediately asked to talk to one of the country's leading gymnasts - Steve.

I was told to meet him in the physio rooms, but the only spare one had piles of glitzy leotards piled up on the desk. I was looking at them when Steve walked in.

We shook hands, and he took a seat.

"These are gorgeous," I said, by way of small talk. "I might have been more interested in the sport if the leotards had looked like this when I was younger. Our school leotards were plain navy."

"Wow, that's a nice thought?"

"What is?"

"You in a leotard."

"Oh, thank you," I said, a bit taken aback by the compliment. I smiled at him, and he smiled back.

"I understand there's concern about your flexibility in the hip area," I said.

"Yeah, I feel fine but need to loosen it out a bit."

"Sure," I replied. "Do you want to lie down on here, and I'll take a look?"

I'll admit it was embarrassing, feeling in and around his hips and groin muscles. There were a few moments when I was handling his hip flexors when he looked at me and smiled. We were both aware of the proximity of my hands. I could also see how well-built he was by the large erection growing under his gym kit. Those clothes don't hide very much.

"Do you need to take a break?" I asked.

"I'm fine," he said, going a delicate shade of pink.

When I'd finished, he sat up.

"Do you fancy going out for a drink tonight? There's no training tomorrow," he replied. "It would be lovely to get to know you better since we're going to spend a lot of time together, and you seem intent on getting very intimate with me very quickly."

"Ha, ha. That's my job!" I said. "I promise I'm not doing anything underhand."

"So, a drink?"

"Yeah, sure, that would be nice."

When we met the next night, it was lovely. We talked about gymnastics, and he mentioned again how wonderful he thought I would look in a leotard. I was in pretty good shape back then, but very few people over 20 look good in a leotard.

Steve talked about all the training they did, we discussed our favourite gymnasts, and he asked me about the other famous sportspeople I'd worked with. The evening went by quickly, and very soon, they were signalling last orders.

"Why don't we get room service," he said.

"To the bar?"

"No, silly. We could go to my room and have something to eat."

"We could just eat here."

"The kitchen's closed, but they'll serve in the rooms."

"Oh, OK. Sure," I said.

It's rare for me to say this, but the truth is that I was hungry, not horny. I fancied a club sandwich or something before hitting the road. And Steve was good company – I enjoyed talking about gymnastics.

We walked to his room and sat on the small sofa under the window. It wasn't a large suite like those participating in more lucrative sports enjoy. Just a standard hotel room. He sat next to me, and I found my eyes travelling down to his legs - sold muscle clad in denim.

We'd had such a lovely evening, and it hadn't felt sexual until then. There had been no holding hands or flirting; we'd been chatting about the AIS and how it compared to the set-up in English sport.

But everything changed when we sat on that sofa, legs touching. I looked at him, and he grabbed me and kissed me. My God, the man could kiss. He pushed his body close to mine as our lips joined. His hands travelled all over my body. I could feel his longing, and it stirred feelings in me.

"You are very naughty," I said. "We came here for food."

"I will order you any food your heart desires if you do something for me," he said.

"Sure."

"Please, will you wear a leotard with those high heels?"

"Really?"

"I'd love that so much."

"OK, I said, but I was slightly wary of the request. He was hanging around with women in leotards all day; wouldn't it be a nice change to be with someone who wasn't wearing a leotard?

As soon as I'd said 'OK' to his request, I could see how excited he was. He pulled me in close again and kissed me passionately, nibbling at my lip, his breathing louder and deeper, his hands caressing my bum cheeks.

"The leotard is on the table," he said.

I went and took it and walked into the bathroom to put it on. Looking back on the scenario now, I don't know why he had a leotard there or why it was lying on the table, ready for me. Presumably, he had planned it?

He certainly enjoyed the whole thing. He almost

lost his mind when I walked out in the leotard, my high strappy sandals and nothing else (I'd dispensed with underwear entirely; there didn't seem to be any point in pretending to myself that any of this clothing would be staying on me for more than five minutes).

"Oh God, you look better than I could ever have imagined," he said, coming up to me and putting his hands on my shoulders. He had rough hands, calloused from the rings and high bar; they felt tough and manly. He turned me round to look at me from behind, then dropped his chin onto my shoulder and kissed my neck. I was dying to turn round, but he held me firmly before hooking his fingers under the straps of the leotard and pulling it down. The leotard was by my waist, and my large breasts bounced free. Steve's hands came round and held them, and I sighed in appreciation.

"My God, you have lovely big tits," he said, pushing himself into the back of me. He carried on massaging my breasts, and I jutted them out further, arching my back and pushing my hips back into him; I could feel his cock pushing against my back.

"Turnaround," he instructed. I turned around slowly and looked into his eyes. They had gone very dark as they stared at my chest. He couldn't keep his eyes off my breasts, so I gently shook them to tease him.

Then he kissed me.

His kisses were becoming firmer. He pushed his face into mine so I could feel every stubble on his beautiful chin. His tongue pushed down into my mouth, and his hands clenched my buttocks, pulling me towards him.

"Take it off," he said.

"But I don't have any panties on," I replied coquettishly.

"Off. Now," he said.

I wiggled out of the leotard, making a real show of shaking and wiggling so that my curves danced before him.

"Sit down," he said.

I sat down firmly on the sofa, making sure I jiggled one more time, and my breasts bounced before him.

"Open your legs."

I opened them wide while still staring at him.

"Come on, big boy," I said, teasing my nipples with my fingers. He immediately moved towards me and rubbed his fingers gently against my clit.

"So wet," he said.

I knew I was wet; I wanted him so much. Strangely, the whole performance of putting on the leotard and standing in front of him - the way he'd stared at me, the passion of his kisses and the intensity of his gaze…it had left me dying to be fucked.

"Get your clothes off," I said, helping him tear them off and watching his body revealed to me in all its muscular glory. He had a much bigger penis than I thought he would. It was large, wide, and sticking out, looking straight at me.

"Come and sit on top of me," he said. "Straddle me, facing me," he commanded.

I wanted nothing more than to feel that large cock in me, so I clambered on top, desperate for those sexy feelings to rush through me. But I wanted to play a little more, so I held back while he tried to manoeuvre himself so that I was riding him. I took his hands and held them up over his head, letting my breasts dangle into his face, he moaned as he sucked on my nipples, and I teased his cock by rubbing my wet pussy up and down against it. "I need to be inside you," he said. "Oh God, I'm going to cum. Now. I want to fuck you."

I dropped onto him and felt him deep within me. Oh God, it was good. I felt so full. So completely fucked. I arched my back so my clit would rub against him as I rode backwards and forwards and fondled my breast. He watched me, teeth bared. We were like two fucking wild animals riding each other in the dead of the night. It was fast, furious and delicious. I rode him vigorously, my nails digging into him, desperate to cum. Then I felt the waves of orgasm begin to rock me. I cried out in delight as he threw me over onto my back and fucked me hard and quick, fondling my breasts, pushing himself inside me until we both screamed out - abandoning ourselves to the wonderful feelings of good, hard sex.

Fuck me, that was good.

NB: In a post-coital stupor, we discussed having sex on every piece of gymnastics equipment and how he would strap me to the bars and fuck me like an animal. But it never happened. Alas. But I love the sport. It brings back such happy memories.

GETTING WET

*M*any of the men I encountered while working as an international physio pursued me cautiously. It was usually a gentle, slow-burning thing.

In the pages of this book, with the encounters listed one after the other, it might sound as if I was having sex with everyone I met, but it wasn't like that. I sometimes worked with these guys for weeks, months, or even years before anything happened.

It was all very slow because they weren't sure whether to approach me, and I wasn't sure whether I should be doing what I was doing. Well, let's be honest: I knew with absolute certainty that I should not be doing what I was doing, but I'd always take a while to wonder whether this would be the end of my career. Was this one a step too far? But sport is a world of incredible, fit, young bodies, and there is a lot of sex around. I worked at three Olympic Games, and everyone was fucking everyone. I was positively prudish compared to many of the officials, coaches, medics and judges who milled around. I certainly wasn't the worst culprit by a long way. Whenever I stopped to think about whether I should get involved, I decided that I wanted sex too much to care. That sounds silly for someone who is desperately ambitious, but the truth is that I love sex. I'm madly oversexed…I don't particularly want cuddles, I don't want loving sex, I want naughty, shouldn't be doing this, sort of sex. That's what I got from my naughty encounters through my work.

When I met Simon (made up name, obvs), an Olympic swimmer of great reputation, it was just before the London Olympics.

He'd been training abroad and hadn't seen his girlfriend for months. And, far from ours being a long professional relationship resulting in a night of passion, he told me he wanted me right away. He was totally unsubtle. There was none of the pandering around, offering pretty smiles, and thinking about where it was all going.

I went to see him about a shoulder injury that he had sustained. He was training at a swim centre in Spain with his national squad. I walked into the treatment room to find him already there. He looked at me and said: "Can I be honest? You are fucking gorgeous."

"Wow," I said. "Thank you."

It has to be said that he was gorgeous, too, and I hadn't had sex for around a year (I know!) I'd been so incredibly busy with Olympians and tending to their needs that my burning needs hadn't been met in a long time.

Our eyes locked, and I felt a shiver of excitement. He felt it, too.

"Let's have a look at this shoulder," I said. "Lie on the bed, face down."

"Yeah, we're going to have trouble with me lying face down," he said. "I've got a massive erection."

Without meaning to, I glanced down at his shorts. There it was.

We took a step closer to each other. This was mad. He stroked my hair, and I turned my head slightly and licked his finger provocatively.

"Come with me," he said, leading me into a room on the side of the swimming pool. It was where the coaches gathered to discuss the swimmers. He shut the door, locked it and pushed me against the wall. He was a lot taller than me, sinewy, but with huge shoulders.

"What's your fantasy?" he asked.

"I'd like all the athletes I work with to be fit and well and win Olympic gold."

"That's very good, but you know what I mean. What's your sexual fantasy? What can I do to make you cum?"

"Oh God," I said.

"You want me to make you cum, don't you?"

I stared, hoping that I could answer his question by looking deeply into his lovely blue eyes. I kept getting flashes back to when I had two footballers simultaneously. I'd love to sleep with two men again, but that wasn't the response he was after.

"I'd quite like to have sex in the water," I said. It wasn't a fantasy but something I fancied doing.

He leaned down and kissed me. "Follow me."

We left the room and headed for the poolside. He went to the far side and locked the door leading to the pool. "There's a chance that someone will have a key and come in, but it's unlikely. It's only used by cleaners, and they aren't here for hours."

"I think it will be worth the risk," I said, undoing the buttons on my physio's shirt and taking it off.

I watched Steve take in the sight of me. I've mentioned my breasts several times in this book, but they are my killer asset. They are very large for my small frame and point upwards; they bounce a lot and are firm. Most importantly, men seem to fall apart when they see them.

He was the same. "You have the best fucking tits ever," he said.

"Touch them."

He moved in and held them, massaging them until my nipples stood out, pink and sharp.

"Mmmmm…that's nice," I said.

"I'm so horny," he replied.

He hadn't even kissed me, which made the whole thing more thrilling.

"Come on. Let's get in," I said.

He jumped into the water, and I made a show of sitting on the side of the pool and then rolling over so that my bum cheeks were fully exposed to him. He came up behind me and took them in his hands, spreading them wide and kissing the mound that contained my throbbing clit.

He dropped me into the water, still facing away from him, and he was at my breasts again…his hands hungrily exploring them.

I turned myself around to face him. Tracing my fingers around the tattoo he sported. Then I reached for his cock and began to tease him. He pushed me up against the metal steps and moved his hand down, pushing my legs apart roughly as he panted and made rocking motions with his hips. "I want you," he said.

He pushed my legs further apart and teased me until I could feel the sensations rise inside me.

"Fuck me," I said. I saw a smile playing across his lips.

Perhaps he wasn't used to women being quite so forward.

"Fuck me now, and fuck me hard," I said. He grabbed and pulled me through the water, dragging me down to the shallow end, kissing me and then pushing himself inside me. It was an odd sensation being in a swimming pool, but the sight of us turned me on; the water thrashing around us as we fucked. I've done it in the sea before, and I have done it in a bath before now, but never in the swimming pool, and it felt quite strange. He pulled my hand above my head and sucked on my nipples as he fucked away at me, the water lapping up, slipping higher and further, slapping up against the wall as we fucked and fucked. I didn't cum, but I loved every minute of it. I liked the roughness, the riskiness and how we were both desperate for it.

GREAT SEX WITH A
HOLLYWOOD STAR

I was invited to work in Memphis in the lead-up to a big fight in which two well-known heavy-weight boxers would be squaring up to one another to become the world's undisputed heavyweight champion. A lot of belts were at stake. This was a big deal. There were also a lot of strong fighters on the undercard, so they tended to swamp the arena with medics at these fights, just to be sure. When something goes wrong in boxing, it can be catastrophic.

So, I went to the USA for six weeks to be based in and around the British boxer's camp. I would be on hand for strapping, assisting with tweaks and minor niggles and also looking after the opponents he was sparring against in practice.

There was a huge contingent, and I couldn't see

how I'd fit in. Obviously, the boxers have teams who work with them constantly, as well as roving medics with particular areas of expertise and surgeons on hand in case of emergencies. I'd been seconded because I was an established and experienced sports physio listed at the Association of Chartered Physiotherapists.

On my first day, I reported to the camp doctor and saw how he looked me up and down. "Hello, what do we have here?" he said.

I told him my name, and he smiled. "Well, I'm very glad to have you here. I might keep you with me."

I know what you're thinking, but I didn't end up in the ring with him. I ended up with someone much, much more famous than him!

I had to follow the doc round and be introduced to everyone. They were a fairly rough bunch.

"Hello, sweetie, wanna massage me? If I tell you where it hurts, will you rub it better?" and all that sort of thing. The sort of language that was fine back then, but you'd be jailed if you used it now.

I loved boxing as a sport then, and I love it now, but I didn't enjoy the six-week stint in Memphis. There were days when I wasn't needed, and when I was involved, it was all very 'wink, wink; nudge, nudge.' I was usually very good at ignoring talk like that, getting my head down and getting on with the job, but not on this trip. When I wasn't needed, I kept away.

Instead, I made the most of my time...I went to see Elvis's house, Graceland, the Mississippi River, and other sites in south Tennessee.

I went off to find Sun Studio because everyone told me it was a must to go there - it was where Chuck Berry, Johnnie Cash and Elvis recorded, the Rock'n'Soul Museum and the Blues Hall of Fame. I'd never done so much sightseeing. Before long, it was the week of the big fight, and there was real tension in the air.

After the weigh-in, I was asked to help with the taping up of the British boxer for the press conference sparring session. I was the only female physio there, and I don't know whether they thought having a woman there with him would bring the hot-headedness down a bit. I went along and helped with strapping. The boxer was a joy....a real gentleman. He asked me what other sportsmen I'd worked with, and I ran through some of them. Like all successful people, he was keen to know about other successful people and to learn from them. He was like a sponge...soaking up any information I could give him.

Once it was done, he punched into his hand so hard that it made me jump. I can only imagine what it must feel like to have that fist coming for your face at 30mph (apparently, that's the speed at which these guys punch!)

I left the room, miles away, still thinking about what a nice guy he was... and walked straight into a Hollywood celebrity and his entourage.

"Is he in there?" asked the famous actor, let's call him Charles. I said he was, but he'd just been strapped and was doing a photocall in the ring.

"Where should we wait?" asked one of the men on the team.

"Sorry, I don't know. He'll be out in the ring for the shoot. Maybe go there?"

"I've got a Hollywood star here; I'm not going to march him into a media scrum," said one of the guys with him.

"I'm a physiotherapist. I have no idea where Hollywood stars are supposed to go," I said, quickly moving towards the exit without making eye contact with anyone.

"Excuse me," came a voice that was so familiar to me; it was like a friend was calling me. I turned around, and the famous actor stood before me.

"Sorry," he said. "There was no need for anyone to speak to you like that. I guess we're just a bit lost."

"I'm not sure where to send you," I said. "The media are everywhere today."

"Where are you going?"

"To the medical room," I said.

"Can I come?" he asked.

"Sure," I said. "There's not much there, though."

HE CAME to the medical room, and we went in and had a coffee. His entourage stood outside. He was lovely company, and though I was initially slightly nervous talking to someone I'd seen in so many films, I soon relaxed. It was odd because I wasn't sure why he was there.

He then said he had to go. I didn't understand why he bothered to come. It was the oddest thing. Then he pulled a card out of his pocket, and I realised it was a ticket.

"Come to this party after the fight," he said. "It's at Sam's Casino."

"Oh," I said. "Thank you."

"It'll be fun. Lots of the guys are going. Michael Jackson, Ben Affleck, Leo Di Caprio, and Tom Cruise will be there. They are all flying in for the fight."

"Wow. OK. Thank you."

Then his phone rang. It was a call from Hugh Heffner, who was in town with half a dozen Playboy Bunnies.

"I better get this," he said. "See you at the party."

I had no intention of attending the party, but then the British boxer won, and everyone was drinking and dancing. Most of them were heading to the party, so I tagged along.

It was a very fancy do...way too posh for my

tastes. Lots of painfully skinny women dripping in jewels and men who were far too smooth for their own good. I went up to the bar to get a drink and managed to lose the group I was with, so I wandered around like a lost soul for a while, thinking that I might head home. It's awful when you're standing around like a lemon with no one to talk to, wondering whether to edge your way into a group.

Then I felt a hand on my shoulder. It was Charles, the famous actor. Everyone turned to look. There were many well-known people there that night, but he was the most famous and attracted lots of glances as he stood close to me. He wore a tuxedo and smelled of wealth and fame. I was excited by the glances and how he squeezed my shoulder as he spoke.

"Thanks for coming," he said. Then he was gone. Off into the crowds, leaving me standing there.

I managed to catch up with a few people I knew, and it was a great party for people-watching, but it was odd to be there and not know anyone, so I headed towards the door.

"Woah, hang on a minute, we haven't even danced yet," said Charles, running towards me, twirling me around and guiding me back into the room.

"I don't know anyone," I said.

"You're the most beautiful woman here; everyone would be happy to make your acquaintance. I had to stop you from leaving us," he said.

I smiled at him. "How did you know I was going?"

"I've been watching you all night," he said.

"You've been watching me?"

"I've been watching how your dress curves around your hips, and your breasts are straining across the fabric at the front. I've been watching you, and you're beautiful. I'm very attracted to you."

"Oh," I said, genuinely surprised. He must have been 20 years older than me and was a Hollywood superstar.

"Why don't we find a table?" he said.

He led me to a booth in the far corner of the room, tucked away and out of sight. His arm was around my waist as we walked.... nothing too aggressive, just enough to assure me he was interested.

We sat next to one another, sipping our drinks and becoming more flirty by the minute. He asked me what sort of men I liked, and I told him I liked older men. That's not true, but I wanted to be desired by him; I wanted to tease and tempt him.

"Why older men?" he asked.

"I like experienced men who know what they're doing."

At that point, I reached over and rested my fingertips on his hand, glancing at it as if looking for something. From there, it was all a formality, a politely flirtatious conversation about the world, neither wanting to appear too eager or anxious. At the same time, we both knew what was going to happen. He moved closer to me, and I pressed up close to him.

He stared straight at me, his face inches from mine and embraced me firmly, with one arm low around the small of my back. I could feel his every breath.

I had an unsettling, nervous sensation in my stomach that I get when I'm ready for sex. A slight tremor ran down my spine; this was slow, intimate, sensual foreplay.

"Would you like to get out of here, you know, go somewhere a little more private?" he asked.

Finally!

"Do you know a place we can go?"

"I have a suite here. The best suite," he said.

We walked out through a private back door swung open for us by security staff, and as soon as we were on our own, I stood in front of him, raised myself on my toes and kissed him: a slow, soft, lingering kiss.

Now there was a special kind of excitement; I was following a Hollywood superstar to his apartment where, hopefully, we would screw each other's brains out.

I knew I was ready for this. I was all prepared - no body hair existed below my eyebrow, and I wore delicate lingerie and stockings with lacy elastic tops.

With his arm behind my back and his hand on my hip, we stepped into the lift and headed to his room.

We walked in without speaking, and I put my bag on the beautiful glass coffee table next to an enormous sofa and sat down. He poured us some champagne and sat down next to me, and I kind of leaned against him as he put his arm around my shoulders. We sat there sipping our drinks and making small talk. I didn't know when he was going to make a move. Then he leaned over towards me to kiss me. It was firmer than I expected, much firmer than the earlier kiss we'd shared, and his tongue was in my mouth almost immediately. I could feel my heartbeat speeding up and a tightening sensation in my breasts as my nipples began hardening. And then there was that peculiar, slightly quivery feeling in my abdomen that I get during arousal.

When our lips separated, I felt his fingertips brush softly across my cheek and up to my forehead, lightly sweeping my hair aside before kissing me on the neck, moving down to the hollow of my throat, sending chills through me every step of the way. Then he began gently nibbling on my earlobe; I heard myself moan.

His hand rubbed my knee, slowly moving up my inner thigh, caressing me. His hand went past the lacy stocking top; my stomach tightened when it touched my flesh. I was glad I wore stockings; the sensation was electric. His hand lingered there, caressing the sensitive flesh of my upper inner thigh before moving on. I inhaled sharply when he began rubbing my pussy through the fabric of the crotch of my panties.

Removing his hand from my crotch, he reached up and pulled my dress off.

When he turned back to me, I tried to strike as coquettish a pose as possible. Reaching over my shoulder, I unhooked my bra, pushed the straps off, and let it fall to my lap.

He groaned at that stage, then kissed me. While our tongues sensuously stroked each other, his free hand cupped my breast, gently massaging and jiggling it with his palm pressed against my erect nipple. A wave of erotic sensations engulfed me. He kissed down from my lips to my chin, upper throat, and lower throat, finally reaching my breasts.

His tongue began deliciously tantalising my nipples one at a time, circling them, flicking back and forth across them, and just plain licking them. He then started kissing and sucking on them. One of his hands slipped into my panties, caressing my pussy, slipping between the lips, finding my clitoris, and gently pressing down on it. I slumped back on the couch, moaning softly, virtually helpless. I was rubbing my hand on his back, over his shirt. Somewhere in my mind, I wondered why he was still wearing his shirt. But as his finger continued to manipulate my clitoris, I stopped worrying about it as I became even more aroused, losing myself in the sensual delights. He began kissing his way back up, retracing his earlier downward trail: cleavage, throat, chin, lips.

I needed to get his clothes off him...tugging at his belt, I unbuckled it and pulled off his trousers. I reached in and took his erect cock in my hand, squeezing it tightly. It was his turn to lean back as I slowly moved my hand up and down. He was erect, strong, and panting with desire. I kissed down his body and ran my lips up and down the shaft, kissing and licking as I went. When I heard him groan, I knew it was time to get serious.

I paused long enough to kiss the head again, then took his cock into my mouth as deep as I could without gagging and began to move my head up and down slowly. All the while, my tongue ran insanely wild, caressing the length of his hard-on as my mouth moved up and down. Then there was a jerk as a slither of cum shot into my mouth. I swallowed quickly. He was almost there.

"Why don't we go into the other room?" he asked. "It'll be more comfortable."

Breathless, all I could do was nod my head. He

opened the bedroom door and guided me. Closing the door, he stepped up behind me and wrapped his arms around me. The room was dark except for an ethereal glow from a bedside lamp.

"Sit down," he said, then he swung around off the bed and onto his knees in front of me. He put his hands on my hips and kissed my naval, the tip of his tongue tickling me exquisitely. I raised my legs, and he bent down, kissing me lightly on my bare inner thighs, and then his tongue traced a path up to my waiting pussy. He kissed each outer lip before slipping his tongue into the gap between them, where it moved upwards to my clitoris. When it made contact, I inhaled in a short series of shallow, sudden, jerking gasps. I came off my elbows and laid flat on my back, my hands now grabbing the bedsheets and clutching them tightly.

I laid there on my back, my knees pulled back as far as I could, breathing irregularly, being deliciously tortured by his tongue. While his tongue swirled and stroked me, he pushed a finger into me, wriggling it and moving it in circular motions, then withdrawing it. But all the time, either tongue or finger attended to my clitoris, driving me erotically forward. I could feel something build up inside me that needed a release, and that release came in the form of a crushingly intense orgasm.

My teeth clenched, I moaned like a wounded animal before emitting a series of gasping sob-like groans as my lower torso seemed wracked with spasms. When it all began to subside, I lay there limply. Then he stood up; his cock was fully erect. I moved to the centre of the mattress. He climbed next to me, ran his hands over my breasts, and bent over and kissed me. I could taste myself on his lips and tongue. I began stroking his cock and balls. He responded by moving down to kiss my breasts. The same tongue that had so adeptly worked on my clitoris was now doing the same for my nipples, pressuring them and flicking its way back and forth across them, reawakening the feelings that had just begun to fade. One of his hands rubbed my pussy; I wanted him inside me.

HE MOVED INTO POSITION, pausing for one last kiss. Then he pushed his cock into me and moved his hips forward gently, taking long, slow, easy thrusts. I wrapped my legs around him, crossing my ankles behind him. I twisted my hips from side to side, meeting his every forward move with a grinding motion, putting an ever-changing pressure on my pussy and stress on my swollen clitoris. My orgasm began to rise again, building up.

As he continued drilling into me, I felt sensations

overtake me; I threw my head back. I heard myself whine out something unintelligible. He sped up his thrusts, humping furiously. He gave a couple of sudden hard deep thrusts into me, each punctuated by the feel of the pulsation of his cock, signalling he was cumming inside me.

THE SEXY AUSTRALIAN IS BACK

J was so excited. Fleur was coming to London en route to the World Athletics Championships, and we'd arranged that she would pop in and see me and stay the night. I'd seen her since my wonderful trip to the AIS many years previously, and we'd stayed in touch and worked at some of the same events over the years, but we'd seen nowhere near as much of one another as we'd have liked. We never seemed to have quality time to sit down and chat properly.

I'd made loads of delicious food, had a fridge full of wine, and anticipated a great, girly catch-up.

I was just sliding the casserole dish into the oven and setting the timer when I heard footsteps at the front door. It was a pleasant late summer's day, so the front door was open to cool the house while I cooked.

"Come in," I shouted as I finished fiddling with the cooker. I heard footsteps, but when I turned, it was Greg standing there instead of Fleur.

Yes. That Greg!

Greg from the garden.

Greg from topless on the bench.

"Wow, smells amazing," he said. "Is there enough for me?"

"Of course," I said. He looked great...he'd hardly changed since our liaison a few years previously. "It's great to see you."

He wrapped me in a delicious hug, lifting me off the ground. "You look as bloody gorgeous as ever. This is for you..."

He handed me a bag containing three bottles of lovely Australian wine, the wine I had fallen hopelessly in love with when I worked out there.

"Stick them in the fridge over there and bring out the one that's in there. Let's finish that first. Where's Fleur?"

"She's not coming. Well, that's not true, she's coming tomorrow. She had to stay in Berlin. She was going to get a later flight but couldn't. She said she tried to call."

"Oh damn. I haven't got my phone here; it's charging upstairs. Is she OK? There aren't any problems, are there?"

"No," he said. "Everything's fine. Just more work there than she expected."

"Oh."

"Is it OK if I stay tonight?" asked Greg.

My world shifted a little on its axis. He was staying. Just the two of us. I never imagined seeing him again, let alone spending the night with him. This was going to be fun.

"Of course, it's OK," I said. "It's very OK."

He looked at me; I looked at him, and – I swear to you –I switched the oven off immediately because I knew we wouldn't be eating.

He refilled my glass, and we walked into the sitting room together. I felt light-headed and girlish in his company. It was so strange. I was no stranger to sexual encounters with men (as you are well aware), but I felt flustered.

"Do you remember us on that bench in Canberra," he said.

"Of course I do. It's not the sort of thing you forget, is it?"

We looked at one another.

"Every time I go near that bench, I think of you," said Greg.

"Tell me what you think of," I said.

"I think of your soft skin, gentle smile, and the knowing look you gave me. The pull of your dress across your chest. I remember seeing those large breasts for the first time. I remember touching them, sucking your nipples and wanting to be inside you. Then I remember that evening when we finally got to be alone. I remember us in the garden shagging like teenagers."

"It was great," I agreed.

Greg moved towards me and wrapped his arms around my neck. His hands were cold from his wine, and I shivered as they touched my shoulder.

"You are so fucking gorgeous," he said, kissing me.

He wore a white shirt with the sleeves expertly folded to the crook of his elbow, exposing his lovely forearms. The thick, dark blond hairs on his arms suddenly took me back in time. I almost felt the sun on my back and heard the ocean...I could almost feel the bench beneath us. He wore dark, slim-fitting jeans with a smart leather belt.

I began to open the buttons on the shirt as he kissed me more passionately, stroking his hairy chest and moving to undo his belt.

As I removed his shirt, Greg slid his hand up my inner thigh under my skirt and ran his knuckles along the crotch of my underwear. "Hmm..."

I bit my lip to diffuse the moan oozing out of me.

He slid his fingers into my panties, rubbing slowly up and down, and he kissed me much more deeply than before as he slid one finger into me.

"Fuuuuck, yes, keep going just like that."

"Just like that?" he teased. "Or maybe a little more?" He kissed my neck as he slid a second finger inside.

"Yes, yes, yes," I panted. "That's perfect."

"Let's get rid of these," he said, and I raised my hips and let him slide my underwear right off. As I rested on the sofa, he looked straight between my legs with a wild glint in his eye.

He dropped to the floor and kissed my thighs, moving up them gently at first, with kisses and soft licks along the crook of my groin, teasing out streams of shivers and shudders that made my lower back spasm and my hips quake. He gradually made his way closer and closer until finally, he was there, his tongue flicking across my clit.

I gripped down on the edges of the sofa as he homed in on my clit, tracing wet, concentrated circles around it; then he thrust two, then three, fingers back into me while his tongue moved faster, and I thrust my hips at him, arching my back and moaning.

"Oh, fuck, that is so good."

Delicious tension was building inside as I wriggled and squirmed.

He reached up and grabbed my breast, squeezing my nipple aggressively.

I reached out for his cock and stroked him with a gentle, firm hand.

"Fuck, I am so wet for you right now."

"Good," he growled, climbing onto me and pushing himself inside. He groaned and dragged me up into him by my hair, pulling me flush to his body as he pumped a little harder and deeper into me until the orgasm came and overtook me. I slumped onto the sofa.

"That's just for starters," he said. "Lots more where that came from…"

MORE SEXY TALES TO COME...

*S*o, there we are then...

I HOPE you've enjoyed this little foray into the world of sport and sportsmen.

There are many more tales to tell...like the times I went on tour with two football sides and one rugby team, but those tour tales will have to wait.

Then there are all my wonderful experiences at the Olympic Games.

They deserve a separate book, all of their own.

If you want to join the newsletter to receive updates when new books are out, please email **anony mousladypublishing@gmail.com,** and I'll make sure you're the first to hear.

You can join our private Facebook group to hear more juicy stories and contribute any of your own:

https://www.facebook.com/groups/ 314840094340400

In the meantime, have fun.

Don't do anything I wouldn't, and keep away from sportsmen - they are nothing but trouble.

xx

Printed in Great Britain
by Amazon

28979180R00091